UNION WITH CHRIST
AND THE
LIFE OF FAITH

SOTERIOLOGY AND DOXOLOGY

Kent Eilers and Kyle C. Strobel, Series Editors

Atonement and the Life of Faith
by Adam J. Johnson

Glorification and the Life of Faith
by Ashley Cocksworth and David F. Ford

Union with Christ and the Life of Faith
by Fred Sanders

UNION WITH CHRIST AND THE LIFE OF FAITH

Fred Sanders

Baker Academic
a division of Baker Publishing Group
Grand Rapids, Michigan

© 2025 by Fred Sanders

Published by Baker Academic
a division of Baker Publishing Group
Grand Rapids, Michigan
BakerAcademic.com

Printed in the United States of America

All rights reserved. No part of this publication may be reproduced, stored in a retrieval system, or transmitted in any form or by any means—for example, electronic, photocopy, recording—without the prior written permission of the publisher. The only exception is brief quotations in printed reviews.

Library of Congress Cataloging-in-Publication Data

Names: Sanders, Fred, 1968– author.
Title: Union with Christ and the life of faith / Fred Sanders.
Description: Grand Rapids, Michigan : Baker Academic, a division of Baker Publishing Group, [2025] | Series: Soteriology and doxology | Includes bibliographical references and index.
Identifiers: LCCN 2024059594 | ISBN 9781540961723 (paperback) | ISBN 9781540967848 (casebound) | ISBN 9781493446322 (ebook) | ISBN 9781493446339 (pdf)
Subjects: LCSH: Mystical union. | Christian life. | Public worship. | Theology, Doctrinal.
Classification: LCC BT767.7 .S36 2025 | DDC 234—dc23/eng/20250215
LC record available at https://lccn.loc.gov/2024059594

Unless otherwise indicated, Scripture quotations are from The Holy Bible, English Standard Version® (ESV®), copyright © 2001 by Crossway, a publishing ministry of Good News Publishers. Used by permission. All rights reserved. ESV Text Edition: 2016

Baker Publishing Group publications use paper produced from sustainable forestry practices and postconsumer waste whenever possible.

25   26   27   28   29   30   31   7   6   5   4   3   2   1

Contents

Series Preface   vii

Preface   xi

Doxological Prelude: Anima Christi   *1*

1. The Creed in Christ   3
   Doxological Interlude: Ephesians 2:4–7   27

2. Scripture in Christ   29
   Doxological Interlude: Three Mysteries (Saphir)   51

3. Variations on a Soteriological Theme   53
   Doxological Interlude: Three Unions (Polhill)   89

4. Union with Christ as Trinitarian Soteriology   91
   Doxological Interlude: "I Cannot Nearer Be" (Bonar)   121

5. Union with Christ and the Christian Life   123
   Doxological Postlude: "Thou Hidden Source" (Wesley)   143

Bibliography   145

Scripture Index   151

Subject Index   153

Series Preface

And Moses said, "Here I am."

Exodus 3:4

IN THE WILDERNESS, Moses stumbles upon a burning bush that somehow goes unconsumed. As if the scene is not arresting enough, the God of his forefathers bellows forth from that crackling, glowing bush: "Moses, Moses!" The response of Moses is simple and yet so evocative of a faithful response to God's call: "Here I am." Holy Scripture pictures that response time and again. So many other encounters with God are unmistakably echoed and foreshadowed here: those of Samuel, Mary, Jesus, and of course Adam. To Adam, God calls, "Where are you?" and he hides, and his hiding is paradigmatic of us all, sadly (Gen. 3:8–10); *but* Moses, Samuel, Mary, and Jesus *offer themselves* in response to the gracious calling of God: "Here I am, Lord." Their proclamation inspires what this series humbly attempts to accomplish: theological activity that bears witness to God's work in time and space to redeem and restore by following the doxological pattern of Moses. Addressed by God and fearful to look upon God's face, Moses finds himself suddenly shoeless in God's holy presence.

Said more formally, the volumes in the Soteriology and Doxology series offer specifically theological interpretations of the Christian life through the lens of various features of God's gracious activity to save, in which doctrinal activity is suffused with and held together by praise. The *gracious acts of God* are the contemplative aim of the series, advancing Christian rationality in grateful response to the redemptive, restorative, and transformative work of the Father by the Son and the Spirit. Focusing on soteriological loci, the topics addressed follow a twofold inclination: that God is the ever-present, captivating reality of all theological work, and that this focus awakens a doxological response that is intrinsic to the proper mode of theological reflection. As such, the orientation of each volume is both dogmatic *and* doxological: each particular doctrine is located within an attentive retrieval of the Christian confession, all while demonstrating how theological reflection springs from worship and spills over into prayer and praise. Seeking to be catholic and evangelical, this series draws upon the richness of the whole church while keeping the sufficiency and singularity of the gospel at center.

The books in the series are designed for theologians-in-formation, meaning that the pedagogical aim of each volume is to train student-readers in a form of theological reasoning that unites what often remains painfully separate in Christian theology: doctrine and spirituality, theology and prayer, the church and the academy, the body of Christ and the individual theologian. This series' approach to theology is exemplified by men and women across the Christian tradition, from Athanasius to Benedict, Ephrem the Syrian to Anselm, Bonaventure to Catherine of Siena, and Aquinas to Calvin. However, with the inclusion of theology in the academic disciplines of the modern university, the expectations and norms of theological reasoning have been altered in many quarters: exegesis is sequestered from theology, and dogmatics from doxology. This series offers something different. It seeks to retrieve forms of theological reflection unapologetic about their home within Christian worship and celebratory of their place within the entire Christian tradition.

With the sight of God as the proper aim of theological contemplation—trembling before the descending fire that calls us to bear witness to his presence—each volume seeks to constructively articulate soteriological loci through the broad range of biblical, historical, and contemporary issues with an eye to expositing the Christian life. While the different authors will vary in how they approach these tasks, the overall flow of each volume will follow a broad fivefold movement: (1) creed, (2) scriptural range, (3) comparative soteriology, (4) constructive theology, and (5) the Christian life, along with a doxological prelude and doxological interludes throughout. Having approached the doctrine from the standpoint of the *regula fidei* through creedal reflection; looked to Holy Scripture for the doctrine's content, scope, and form; and measured diverse traditions of biblical interpretation and theological reasoning, each volume offers a contemporary restatement of Christian teaching that shows how this theological locus directs doxology and Christian living. The *lived* reality of Christian existence, often far from the purview of theological reflection, remains the focused end of articulating the saving acts of God.

O the depth of the riches and wisdom and knowledge of God! . . . For from him and through him and to him are all things. To him be the glory forever. Amen. (Rom. 11:33, 36 NRSV)

Kent Eilers
Kyle C. Strobel
Series Editors

Preface

SALVATION, ACCORDING TO CHRISTIAN THEOLOGY, has two moments: *In* and *Christ Jesus*. "A preposition followed by a proper name" is the key to the fullness of what salvation is.[1] The preposition and the name are not equal factors; they do not bear the same weight at all. What's "in" without "Christ Jesus"? The center of gravity is decisively located in the proper name, a compound proper name that includes the person (Jesus) and his title of office (Christ). God accomplishes salvation by means of the person and work of this one, Christ Jesus. "Christ Jesus" indicates something real and full in itself, someone infinitely worthy of knowing, learning about, and following after.

The little preposition "in" can of course scarcely do any work on its own. Isolated, it would be reduced to a cipher, an abstract principle of relatedness, a placeholder suggesting that something is contained by something else. The mere placeholder status of "in" explains why it would be shortsighted to start out by saying that salvation's two moments are the savior and the saved, or by drawing two circles at some distance from each other (representing you and Christ) and then asking how they are to be related. Analytically speaking, there

1. Pierson, *In Christ Jesus*, ix.

are in fact two realities to be accounted for: the one who saves and the one who is saved. But organizing our thoughts around these two circles would run the risk of unproductive juggling. If we instead start by focusing adequate attention on the one who saves, we discover that his reality is so comprehensive as to contain salvation within itself. To describe Christ Jesus is already to offer an account of salvation. We draw one circle, representing Christ Jesus, and alongside it we draw not another circle but an arrow registering "in."

"In" plus "Christ" is the key; the key turns in the lock; the door opens. "A very small key may open a very complex lock and a very large door, and that door may lead into a vast building with priceless stores of wealth and beauty."[2] Soteriology is a vast theological structure, and "in Christ" is what opens it. Entering the domain of soteriology by way of the "in Christ" formula means considering Christ Jesus by way of the doctrine of union with Christ.

When we take up the task of exploring the soteriological theme of union with Christ, we are considering the vast field of Christology, complexly combined with our own inclusion within it. The invitation to consider union with Christ is an invitation to contemplate Christ as our salvation. Carried out with proper attention to its due proportions, this kind of soteriology is mostly Christology. This kind of soteriology, properly centered on the *sōtēr* (savior), is the kind most fully open to doxology, because it is already focused not only on salvation but on the one who is to be praised for salvation.

Nobody can do full justice to the doctrine of union with Christ, but the most insightful treatments of the theme throughout Christian history have in common a certain centripetal energy, a center-seeking tendency that strives to recognize union with Christ as the heart of soteriology. In this brief book, we will sketch out the main implications of that centrality. Our goal is to indicate how the reality of union with Christ shapes the entire doctrine of salvation. Union with Christ is among the broadest categories available for characterizing

2. Pierson, *In Christ Jesus*, ix.

Christian salvation. It transcends the confessional differences among various theological systems because of its utterly basic status. Though it is not at odds with a well-structured *ordo salutis* (as some have mistakenly suggested), it does tend to outflank or overwhelm any structural schema within which we might try to locate it. Union with Christ refuses to nestle snugly into any single slot or to stay put, simply because of its thematic vastness and material comprehensiveness.

This volume on union with Christ delineates the theological context within which we can locate all the other topics and details of soteriology (the estimable doctrines explored by other volumes in this Soteriology and Doxology book series). It argues that the doctrine of union with Christ belongs at the controlling center of soteriology.

The book begins by analyzing the structure of Christian faith itself, as expressed in the Apostles' and Nicene Creeds (chap. 1). Next, we explore the New Testament's witness to union with Christ (chap. 2). In both of these chapters, the point is not so much that we can find the doctrine of union with Christ contained in or taught by the creeds and the Scriptures; rather the point is that the creeds and even the New Testament itself were called into being by the spiritual reality of union with Christ. A comparative chapter then considers some divergent ways that union with Christ has been understood (chap. 3) before we turn to a more constructive account of union with Christ that draws out its inherently trinitarian structure: God the Father has worked out salvation in the incarnate Son and now applies it through the Holy Spirit (chap. 4). The long lines of soteriology stretch down from the unity of the Trinity, through the economic coordination of the missions of the Son and the Spirit, into the church, and from there into the personal experience of Christians (chap. 5). While the understanding and expression of Christian experience varies widely, union with Christ does give it a consistent form. The filial life of Christ the Son, having been worked out in his own incarnation, is replicated in Christian experience. We are formed within his frame. Most concretely, this takes the shape of dying and rising with Christ, which in its churchly articulation shows forth in baptism (the believer immersed into Christ) and the Lord's Supper (Christ being received by the believer). The book concludes by noting how an evangelical emphasis on the experience of regeneration fits nicely within the broad expanse of patristic trinitarian soteriology.

An earlier version of some of the material in this book (especially scattered through the first three chapters) was delivered as the Norton Lectures for 2022 at the Southern Baptist Theological Seminary in Louisville, Kentucky. I thank provost Matthew Hall for the timely invitation to deliver those lectures, and the faculty and students who engaged in conversation with me on union with Christ. I delivered part of chapter 4 as a conference paper ("In Christ in the Trinity: Union with Christ in Trinitarian Perspective") at the 2022 annual meeting of the Evangelical Theological Society in Denver, Colorado. Diligent readers may also find that I have worked out some of these ideas in blog form at my online resource site, fredfredfred.com.

DOXOLOGICAL PRELUDE

Anima Christi

Soul of Christ, hallow
body   strengthen
blood   ransom
water   wash   } me.
stripes   heal
sweat   refresh
wound   hide

From *The Preces Privatae of Lancelot Andrewes, Bishop of Winchester*, translated, with an introduction and notes, by F. E. Brightman (London: Methuen & Co., 1903), 93.

CHAPTER ONE

The Creed in Christ

THE HISTORIC CHRISTIAN CREEDS (Apostles' and Nicene) teach that salvation consists in union with Christ. Nevertheless, the goal of this chapter is not simply to demonstrate that. If we wanted to begin our theology by taking up a primary text as the foundation of teaching about union with Christ, it would be more instructive to turn directly to Scripture, perhaps borrowing a creedal outline to organize the biblical material. Beginning with a historic creed may even run the risk of suggesting that we believe in union with Christ not because it is taught in Scripture but because it is taught by the ancient, historic documents of the church. But recall what it means to have a creed: a creed specifies what we believe by making a concise statement of the content of that belief. Recalling that *credo* means "I believe," I devote this chapter to showing that the structure of the Christian faith reflects salvation by union with Christ. We will see this first in the way the Apostles' Creed organizes itself around union with Christ, and then in the way the Nicene Creed sets this same schema against a more explicitly trinitarian background. But first, precisely because union with Christ is so central to the faith, we will consider the great advantage of having recourse to the historic creeds.

3

"Within Thy Wounds, Hide Me"

While it makes sense to speak about "the Christian doctrine of God" or "the Christian doctrine of the incarnation," it seems less plausible in the contemporary world to assert that there is one single Christian doctrine of salvation. Whatever convergence and agreement there may be in the great, central teachings about God or Christ, these common truths recognized and enshrined in the earliest Christian creeds and liturgies and commentaries, surely when it comes to soteriology there must be more divergence and disagreement. Don't the various branches of Christendom often do their branching out precisely here, over questions of what salvation is? Conventional wisdom holds that the many complex questions that arise here are the very questions over which we divide into varied traditions (say Roman Catholic and Protestant), distinct denominations (say Lutheran and Reformed), and even antagonistic families or tribes (say Calvinist and Arminian, pedobaptist and credobaptist, and so on). So while we would never, in good taste, let ourselves speak of a peculiarly Baptist doctrine of the Trinity (horrors!) or an exclusively Presbyterian doctrine of the incarnation (I shudder), we do sometimes feel that it makes sense to speak of a range or variety of soteriologies. And so we sometimes speak of the Calvinist soteriology, a Wesleyan account of salvation, and so on.

But letting ourselves speak this way can signal an underlying error in our understanding of the faith. To think of Christian traditions as being parceled out and divided up among competing soteriologies is too loose; it illegitimately gives too much importance to the differences within the continuum of belief. Such a taxonomy is too broad and irresponsible to do justice to the actual lay of the land. The soteriological lay of the land, I want to argue, is the domain of the doctrine of union with Christ. There is one Christian soteriology, and that is, by definition, salvation by union with Christ.

Of course there are soteriological differences among Christians and churches. We will consider in chapter 3 the variety of ways in which different theologies understand union with Christ. But the key point here, as we examine the creeds, is that those are differences within the larger context of a broad agreement. This is partly a judgment about scale. If we think of union with Christ in terms of geography, we should think of soteriological disagreements as real estate. And even at that smaller level, we do well to keep a sense of perspective about the difference between large and small parcels of disagreement. Two kinds of Presbyterians may argue about the nature of the covenant; three kinds of Baptists may argue about the status of the law in the Christian life; four kinds of Anglicans may argue about the sacraments. These things matter, but they matter within certain agreed-upon territories of a broader consensus.

Some differences run very deep indeed, and we should be alert to those boundaries that mark the edge of Christian fellowship. If somebody preaches "a different gospel," as Paul warns the Galatians, that gospel is not really a gospel at all (Gal. 1:6–7).[1] In extreme instances, differences in soteriology lead not just to questioning the Christian status of a rival confession but to outright rejection of that status. Consider J. Gresham Machen's critique of systematized theological liberalism as a project that claims to be Christian but that "differs from Christianity in its account of the gospel itself."[2] Machen is in fact reacting against a soteriology so deficient that it fails to be Christian, but the kind of theological liberalism he has in view is also radically deficient "with regard to the presuppositions of the gospel (the view of God and the view of man), with regard to the Book in which the gospel is contained, and with regard to the Person whose work the gospel sets forth."[3] Boundaries exist, and a soteriological system that transgresses them fails to be Christian. But the converse also holds: soteriological systems that don't cross those boundaries are by definition Christian, despite their regional variations.

---

1. J. C. Ryle has a searching chapter on errors that threaten to "spoil the gospel." See "Evangelical Religion."

2. Machen, *Christianity and Liberalism*, 117.

3. Machen, *Christianity and Liberalism*, 117.

We should clearly acknowledge these theological differences, be analytically precise and intellectually honest about them, and learn the procedural rules for how to argue well so that our territorial disputes over matters of the gospel are both vigorous and virtuous. Good fences make good neighbors; unclear boundaries invite border skirmishes; sound theology tends to draw distinctions, not dissolve them. But while most active differences in soteriology are about real estate, union with Christ is geography, the vast and fundamental ground itself. Both require surveying, but the surveys operate at radically different scales. And real estate rests on geography for its solidity, its orientation, and its possibilities of cultivation.

As an illustration of this principle, consider the doxological prelude printed before this chapter. It is a prayer that asks, "Soul of Christ, hallow me; body of Christ, strengthen me; blood of Christ, ransom me," and so on through seven requests. It powerfully sets forth the spirituality of union with Christ. Readers familiar with the prayer and readers seeing it for the first time may have quite similar responses to its vivid appeal. It seems to speak from the heart, articulating the Christian desire to be saved to the uttermost by union with all that is in Christ. The prayer is called the *Anima Christi*, for the first two words in its original Latin. An anonymous prayer, it dates to the fourteenth century[4] and is most familiar in Roman Catholic culture. Here are its impressively Roman Catholic credentials: It has been very popular as a eucharistic hymn and is included in the Roman Missal. Ignatius of Loyola, founder of the Jesuit order, makes use of it in his *Spiritual Exercises*—where the prayer is sometimes given the title *Aspirations of St. Ignatius* and at the popular level is often thought to have been written by Ignatius (though this has long been known to be demonstrably false). A medieval pope declared that penitents who recited it at Mass earned a three-thousand-day indulgence. In the nineteenth century the *Anima Christi* had a surge of popularity and was once again "indulgenced" by Pius IX in 1854. It is, in other words, extremely Roman Catholic.

4. Julian, *Dictionary of Hymnology*, 70.

The Creed in Christ 7

But not exclusively so. Most importantly, there is nothing in the text that is uniquely Roman Catholic or that contradicts Protestant theology. Here is the full text:

> Soul of Christ, sanctify me.
> Body of Christ, save me.
> Blood of Christ, inebriate me.
> Water from the side of Christ, wash me.
> Passion of Christ, strengthen me.
> O Good Jesus, hear me.
> Within Thy wounds, hide me.
> Suffer me not to be parted from Thee.
> From the malignant foe, defend me.
> At the hour of my death, call me,
> And bid me come to Thee,
> That with Thy saints I may praise Thee
> For all eternity. Amen.[5]

The Anglican Lancelot Andrewes (1555–1626) incorporated part of the prayer into his *Private Prayers*; in fact, his clever arrangement of it in abbreviated form is the excerpt printed as our doxological prelude. The bracket gathers together all the requests and makes them converge terminatively on "me." But it was not just among high-church Anglicans that the *Anima Christi* took hold of Protestant hearts. The prayer was translated into German as an expanded rhyming hymn[6] and became popular among various Lutheran Pietist groups. That was where John Wesley picked it up, rendering Johannes Scheffler's "Die Seele Christi heil'ge mich" into English in the form "Jesu, Thy Soul Renew My Own." Here are his first two stanzas:

> Jesu, thy soul renew my own,
> Thy sufferings for my sins atone;

5. Thurston, "Notes on Familiar Prayers: The Anima Christi," 493.
6. Julian, *Dictionary of Hymnology*, 70.

Thy sacred body slain for me
From sin and misery set me free.

The water issuing from thy side
The soldier's spear had open'd wide,
That bathe my heart, and all thy blood
Refresh and bring me near to God.

The journey of the *Anima Christi* from Roman Catholic to Anglican to Lutheran to Methodist circles is instructive. What stays constant is the central idea of salvation by union with Christ, expressed by way of a poetic strategy that itemizes the elements of Christ's death and addresses them almost as personifications. It lists Christ's soul, his body, his blood, the water from his side (*aqua lateris Christi*), and his passion, and to each of these it correlates a soteriological benefit: sanctification, salvation, refreshing, cleansing, strength. The point of distinguishing them poetically is not to parcel them out or to choose among them but to gain a sense of the comprehensiveness of total salvation in Christ. This opening strategy then gives way to a direct prayer addressing Jesus and then to a compelling petition for Jesus to make himself the hiding place of those he saves: "O good Jesus, hear me. / Within Thy wounds, hide me." There could hardly be a stronger or more personal sense of union with Christ than a prayer to be hidden within his wounds. And the final lines look forward to hearing Christ's own voice summon us into eternal praise. If the opening lines seem to dismember Christ into impersonal personifications, the final lines are relentlessly personal and interpersonal.

As the prayer was naturalized or enculturated into the different Christian traditions, it took on local color and accent. The Roman Catholic placement of it in a eucharistic liturgy resonates with the concrete nouns of the opening lines: "body," "blood," "water from the side." These words certainly function well in the context of the Lord's Supper; in a eucharistic setting, the body and blood of the prayer and the body and blood of communion with Christ can recirculate the meaning of salvation in Christ. Roman Catholics furthermore have a very distinctively elaborated theology of the mode of Christ's presence in the elements (transubstantiation). The same words function differently in Lancelot Andrewes's private prayers. Whatever Andrewes's own Anglican sacramentology, his use of the *Anima Christi* was for personal devotion in secret. The Pietists and the Wesleyans refracted the same prayer further. John Wesley made explicit the way Christ's soul heals the soul of the one praying: "Jesu, thy soul renew my own." Nobody else praying the *Anima Christi* had yet mentioned their own soul until the prayer underwent its Wesleyan transformation. The theological differences among those who pray the prayer become more evident the longer one sits with them. Perhaps the well-developed late medieval theology of the human soul of the incarnate God-man is the only possible matrix within which a prayer to the "soul of Christ" could have arisen. And yet, once this prayer about union with Christ was available, it was received in other theological frameworks with subtly differing spiritual emphases. It might even be possible to pick a good theological fight over the meaning of the words of the prayer, if we tried hard enough to draw the differences to the surface and explicate them sharply enough. This is exactly what we would expect, given our commitment to the centrality of union with Christ as the one Christian soteriology. We expect agreement about the main thing (union with Christ) and disagreements about the details.

Creedality and Credibility

There is in fact a common Christian account of what salvation is, and a great deal depends on us learning to see that commonality and to make our approach to that single soteriology even in all the details and complications of our differences, warranted as the differences may be. The one single Christian doctrine of salvation concerns union with Christ; it is characterized by a recognizably Christian way of approaching Christ: paying a particular kind of attention to Christ himself, seeing him for who he truly is, coming to him in need and obedience, and uniting to him. This approach to salvation in Christ is so deeply embedded in the Christian faith that it is the spiritual reality that generated the ancient creeds and guided the ecumenical councils, and it continuously underwrites doctrinal contemplation of salvation in a vast array of classic theological sources and their reception. This chapter will consist of discerning the form of union with Christ in those creeds, councils, and earliest contemplations.

But first, a word on why such an account of union with Christ aims to be simultaneously creedal and credible. It has to do not only with what we believe (creedal) but with whether we are believable (credible). On the face of it, contemporary culture is more inclined to give Christian truth claims a hearing if the truth claims plausibly represent what Christians as a whole believe rather than what just one of the identifiable subsections of Christians believe. Christian claims tend to be more persuasive when more unified; at least, the inquiring secular mind can proceed more directly to entertaining the truth claims of Christian theology if it can skip over the appearance of plurality and difference. The message of salvation, as it comes to people in the world today, would be more plausible if all who claimed the name of Christ agreed on and were eloquent about the same doctrine of salvation. To that extent, our credibility depends a great deal on the effectiveness of our common creedality. We will be more believable if the "we" in "we believe" includes a vast, global, ancient congregating of the faithful. There is a strategic advantage to being able to invite people to consider a Christian faith whose profile is recognizable from a distance.

If you are like most Christians, you prefer all the Christians in the world to reach doctrinal unanimity by agreeing with you. That would in fact solve the problem and produce unity. But while each of us waits patiently for that to happen, we do well not to exaggerate our differences. The power of unified testimony is part of why Jesus prayed—not just for his first disciples but for those who would believe in him through their testimony—"that they may all be one, . . . so that the world may believe that you have sent me" (John 17:21).

The section of the prayer just quoted begins with unity and ends with credible witness. But between those is a section I omitted from the quotation: "just as you, Father, are in me, and I in you, that they also may be in us." That middle section is in fact the crucial link. It connects the unified Christian witness on one side to the world's acceptance of the message on the other. And it is precisely what this chapter takes up in analyzing the faith. Against the deep, all-sufficient background in the unity of the Trinity (the Father in the Son and the Son in the Father, as the Holy Spirit testifies), Jesus sets forth this reality: "that they also may be in us." Here is the invitation to a trinitarian account of our union with Christ.

It is worth mentioning in passing that this great prayer of John 17 articulates a profound theological account of the unity of those who believe in Christ. A trinitarian foundation for the unity of the church is suggested here, and it would be possible to draw that very important theme into the foreground. That trinitarian-shaped unity of the church is in fact a more substantial and more significant topic than what we are currently examining. It is the secret at the center. Here, my only point is that the world beyond the church is more likely to pay attention and find Christian claims plausible if they are set forth with some degree of unanimity. That is all—the more creedal, the more credible.

In taking up the two classic early Christian creeds—the Apostles' Creed and the Nicene Creed—to understand the nature of union with Christ, we are resisting the fairly widespread conventional wisdom that says the early centuries of the church did not have a carefully elaborated view of salvation. In its weakest manifestations, this objection is an ill-informed and lazy wave of the hand at pervasive pluralism, a vague sense that the ecumenical councils were about Trinity and Christology rather than soteriology, leaving us in doubt about what salvation even meant to the early church. But in its strongest form, the observation has more merit. The claim is that the early church did not produce soteriological theory at the doctrinal or theological level because soteriology simply wasn't one of the issues that the early church contested and had councils about. No less an authority on the creeds than J. N. D. Kelly puts it this way:

> The student who seeks to understand the soteriology of the fourth and early fifth centuries will be sharply disappointed if he expects to find anything corresponding to the elaborately worked out syntheses which the contemporary theology of the Trinity and the Incarnation presents. In both these latter departments controversy forced fairly exact definition on the Church, whereas the redemption did not become a battle-ground for rival schools until the twelfth century, when Anselm's *Cur deus homo* (c. 1097) focused attention on it. Instead he must be prepared to pick his way through a variety of theories, to all appearance unrelated and even mutually incompatible, existing side by side and sometimes sponsored by the same theologian.[7]

Kelly's reference to Anselm and an emergent "battle-ground for rival schools" is telling, but we will return to that at a later point. Our immediate task is to take up and read the central texts of the early church's response to Scripture. We begin with the Apostles' Creed and then move to the Nicene Creed.

The Apostles' Creed: Articulated for Union with Christ

The Apostles' Creed has three articles, one for each person of the Trinity.

The first article, on God the Father Almighty, is very short. He created heaven and earth. Much more could be said about God the Father, but it is not said here in the Apostles' Creed. The doctrine of the First Person of the Trinity has never really had a handy name, something parallel to Christology or pneumatology (paterology?). And here in the creed, the statement about faith in the First Person of the Trinity is not elaborated with a series of clauses. We do not get much by way of a recital of attributes or actions. In fact, when the creed confesses faith

---

7. Kelly, *Early Christian Doctrines*, 375.

in "God, the Father almighty, maker of heaven and earth," it provides exactly one attribute (omnipotence) and one action (creation). But neither of these is unique to the Father in the sense of excluding the Son and the Holy Spirit. That is, the Son is also almighty and is also agent of creation. Likewise, coming third in order of mention, the Spirit is also almighty Creator. So what is the Apostles' Creed doing by ascribing this attribute and this action to the Father? It is applying them by way of appropriation. Appropriation is naming a theological move in which an attribute or action belonging equally to the three persons of the Trinity is predicated of one person because, although it belongs to the Godhead as such, it bears an instructive likeness to the personal distinction of that person. That instructive likeness allows us to discern that person's character within the eternal Trinity's relations. In this case, the Father is the person of the Trinity who is the principle of the Son and Spirit. According to the doctrines of eternal generation and spiration, from all eternity the Son and Spirit subsist as being from the Father; they come from him. And this inner-trinitarian consubstantial "coming from," while it is certainly not the same as the world coming from the triune God, is nevertheless instructively like the world coming from the triune God. God's creation, even though it is *ex nihilo* ("from nothing") and enters into temporality, is a kind of gigantic resemblance to the Father's distinct hypostatic character as principle of the Son. The Apostles' Creed thus quietly commandeers the language of the indivisible outer work of the almighty Trinity to give us the opportunity to discern the inner reality of the Father.[8] But it happens in the flash of just a few words: "I believe in God, the Father almighty, maker of heaven and earth." The Apostles' Creed is in a hurry to get to something else.

That something else is the second article, on the Son. The creed's rush to Christology is instructive: nobody knows the Father except the Son. Even though the creed intentionally unspools in serial order, its decision to start with the Father must rapidly give way to the

---

8. McFarland, "'God, the Father Almighty.'"

revelation of the Son. This second article is the longest article in the creed, largely because it tells the story of Jesus: he was conceived by the Spirit, was born of the virgin Mary, suffered under Pontius Pilate, was crucified, died, was buried, descended to the dead, rose again, ascended into heaven, sits at the Father's right hand, and will return to judge. This abbreviated story of the life of Jesus is the center of the creed, a tiny recapitulation of the main points of his life, tracking closely with the outline of the Gospels and even more closely with the brief summaries of the life of Jesus featured in early Christian preaching, such as Peter's sermon in the house of Cornelius in Acts 10.

Though the second article is mostly narrative, it is not all story without remainder. It begins with a cluster of five names or titles: Jesus, Christ, only begotten, Son, Lord. This recital of christological titles concentrates a great deal of biblical vocabulary in a short span, making it easy to memorize. In fact, the Apostles' Creed may have expanded outward from the original confession "Jesus is Lord," according to some theories of historical creedogenesis. We can imagine opening up the primal confession "Jesus is Lord" and inserting between "Jesus" and "Lord" the titles "Christ," "only begotten," and "Son." "Only begotten Son," of course, is the trinitarian anchor that holds the second article to the first. In retrospect, we see that the deepest meaning of "Father" was always "Father of the Son," and now we come to know the Father as such by knowing the Son of the Father.

So a solid foundation of Christology is laid in the names and titles, but what the creed builds on this foundation is the gospel story. The decision to recite the story of Jesus is structurally central to the Apostles' Creed. This brief formula specifying the content of Christian faith and the identity of the Christian God functions to enshrine the irreducible and irreplaceable story in which the identity of the incarnate Son is rendered. So this second article is also the most tightly coherent of the three, precisely because it follows a narrative logic: he was conceived, was born, suffered, died, rose. Obviously much is omitted from the recital: there is nothing between the birth of Jesus and his suffering under Pontius Pilate. The creed skips the thirty-something years of the life of Jesus, including the entirety of his ministry and teaching. Instead it makes a direct line to the cross. The creed goes from Christmas to Easter (or more precisely, Passion Week) in a single bound. And lest we try to offer an excuse for this decision by saying it was based on the need for brevity, the creed then devotes several clauses to that final week: Jesus suffered, was crucified, died, was buried, descended to the dead, and rose again. Why only these? Why all of these? If the second article is viewed merely as summary, the decisions embedded into the creed's selections are peculiar enough to pose the question, What principles drove the selectivity? These are not just the key plot points of a biography; they are theologically motivated inclusions following a soteriological path of reasoning. The logic is soterio-logic. The bundle of events at the end of the earthly life of Jesus meets up with the bundle of titles at his introduction in the creed. The point of the creed is to identify this person and then narrate his death and resurrection.

In terms of selectivity, though, it is the third article of the creed that contains the oddest assortment. It curtly says, "I believe in the Holy Spirit," and then continues with something like a list of various other important things believed: the holy catholic church, the communion of saints, the forgiveness of sins, the resurrection of the body, and life everlasting. While each of these merits close attention and theological elaboration, they seem to lack the kind of inevitability that would make them obvious as a cluster. All of them can fruitfully be contemplated under the heading of pneumatology: the Spirit forms the church, mediates forgiveness, works physical resurrection, and so on. Even so, these are not the five works of the Holy Spirit we would be likely to promote if we were working up a biblical account of pneumatology from scratch, nor are they held together by anything like the narrative logic that guides the second article. But here, in the gap between the second and third articles, is where the formative power of the doctrine of union with Christ exerts itself. Skipping over for a moment the phrases about the holy catholic church and the communion of saints, notice the closing triad: forgiveness, resurrection, and everlasting life. Some Reformation commentators on the creed have noted that these three things mentioned in the third article are prominent benefits of union with Christ.

Because we are in Christ, we have forgiveness of sins, resurrection of the body, and life everlasting. So in that sense, the creed's three articles do the work of articulating (eloquently elaborating) the doctrine of union with Christ by first telling his story and then naming the blessings that flow from it for those who are in Christ. This status of being in Christ is introduced under the governing head of believing in the Holy Spirit. In other words, the second article states, in christological terms, the accomplishment of redemption, and the third article states, in pneumatological terms, the application of redemption.

That is the main point, but the creed's articulation of union with Christ by the work of the Spirit may be even more tightly knit. There is an observable correspondence between three sequential events of the second article and three benefits of the third article. Corresponding to the second article's "I believe that Jesus was crucified" is the third article's "I believe in the forgiveness of sins." Stated backward: Why do I believe in the forgiveness of sins? Because I believe that Jesus was crucified. Corresponding to "I believe that Jesus rose from the dead on the third day" is "I believe in the resurrection of the body." And corresponding to "I believe that he ascended into heaven and sits at the right hand of the Father" is "I believe in life everlasting."

Second Article	Third Article
He was crucified	Forgiveness of sins
He rose on the third day	Resurrection of the body
He ascended into heaven and sits at the right hand of the Father	Life everlasting

It is a compelling alignment between the accomplishing of salvation in Christ and the application of its benefits to believers by the Holy Spirit. The second article is the story of how this redemption is worked out in the life, death, and resurrection of Christ himself; the third article tells how it is worked into the church by the Holy Spirit.

It is easy to think of union with Christ as just one of the things we believe in as Christians. And there is a sense in which that is true; a responsible list of doctrines will include many distinct theological topics, and union with Christ will be only one among many. But union with Christ is an exceedingly expansive doctrine with a strategic role to play in determining the form and the content of Christian faith. The entire creed is wrapped around it, built to enshrine it, or (to reverse the direction of the metaphors) developed out from it. We might think of it this way: we come to the ancient witness to inquire whether union with Christ is in the creed, and we discover that the creed is actually inside of union with Christ, in the sense that the creed is what it is because it arises to articulate redemption accomplished and applied by Christ and the Spirit.

The Nicene Creed: The Trinitarian Identity of the Son

Much of what we have just seen in the Apostles' Creed applies also to the Nicene Creed.[9] In particular, we find in the Nicene Creed a three-article statement of faith in the Father, Son, and Holy Spirit. The first and third articles are carefully gathered around a second article in which, at the heart of the heart of the faith, is a miniature gospel story. In seven or eight points, the story of Jesus Christ is retold. While there are fascinating variations in selection and phrasing between the two creeds, the plot outline is quite obviously similar: conception by the Spirit and birth from Mary; crucifixion, death, and burial; resurrection, ascent, and seating at the Father's right hand.

---

9. The Nicene Creed is widely available. A good scholarly source is Mark DelCogliano's translation from *The Cambridge Edition of Early Christian Writings*, vol. 1, *God*, edited by Andrew Radde-Gallwitz, 268–69. What we popularly call the Nicene Creed is not the Creed of the Council of Nicaea (325) but the Creed of the Council of Constantinople (381). Both texts, along with brief explanations of their histories, are available in the volume of *The Cambridge Edition of Early Christian Writings* cited.

What distinguishes the Nicene Creed, though, is how this narrative christological core is introduced. Instead of introducing Christ with a rapid series of key biblical names and titles, the Nicene Creed goes on to say of the only begotten Son, rather elaborately, that he is "begotten of the Father before all ages" and that he is "begotten, not made." We can think of these two phrases as expanding on what his *monogenēs* sonship means: positively, it is an eternal begetting rather than one bounded by time with a beginning or an end. That is the sense of "begotten of the Father before all ages." Negatively, it is explicitly not creation; though the Son and the world are both from the Father, the fromness that the Son has is absolutely distinct from the fromness the world has. That is the meaning of "begotten, not made." Between these positive and negative specifications of the Son's generation is a kind of poetic pair of phrases that ring the changes on the concept of fromness: "Light from Light, true God from true God." These phrases build on each other, but each of them takes a word or symbol for deity and repeats it, placing in the midst of the repetition the notion of fromness. So the one God is named twice by the same noun, held apart by nothing but the preposition "from." We hear of Light and then again of the same Light (for God is light, 1 John 1:5), but the Light has within itself a relation of fromness. There is a relation internal to the Light that is God. This Son is true God, but in the Nicene way of confessing it, he is true God standing in the relation of being from true God. Finally, the precision of all of this is strategically secured by calling him *homoousios*: of the numerically same nature, consubstantial with the Father.

Because of the controversies of the fourth century, the Nicene Creed goes to great lengths to specify the identity of the Son before it begins to deploy the gospel summary. We might say it displays the same precious christological jewel as the earlier creed but invests much more heavily in securing its setting. And the Nicene Creed has one more addition to make before plunging into the Jesus story. Between the eternal identity of the only begotten Son in the consubstantial Trinity and his incarnation for us and our salvation the

The Creed in Christ   19

Nicene Creed inserts "through him all things were made." The line is, of course, taken from the prologue of John's Gospel (John 1:3), but by deploying it precisely here, the Nicene Creed takes extra care to place the Son on the Creator side of the Creator-creation distinction. A poor reading of the Apostles' Creed might just have been able to take the words in sequence and put the Son on the creature side. After all, wasn't God the Father named first, as almighty maker of heaven and earth, before the Son was introduced? It would be a desperate misinterpretation of the Apostles' Creed, but one that is not explicitly excluded by the text. Not so with the Nicene Creed: all things were made through this Son, and only when that has been reaffirmed does the Nicene Creed go on to give us the story of his incarnate work. Imagine how the creed would flow if the line about creation were not included. In its absence, the Nicene Creed would move directly from "begotten of the Father before all ages, . . . consubstantial with the Father" to "for us and our salvation he came down from heaven . . . and was incarnate and was made human." We could still see the great distinction between who God the Son eternally is by nature and what God the Son freely undertakes to do by grace. Eternally by nature he is the divine Son; freely by grace he assumes human nature to save it. But the inclusion of the line about creation sharpens and clarifies the distinction: the Son's eternal identity is established before, above, and without reference to creation.

The line distinguishing the Son's essential identity from his gracious actions is conspicuously and elaborately present in the Nicene Creed. It runs directly through the center of the second article. It is the clear, bright line between what the church fathers called *theologia* and *oikonomia*, between God's eternal nature and God's work of salvation. It is the most important dividing line in the entire field of Christian theology; it recognizes the deep aseity and absolute self-sufficiency of God while keeping grace truly gracious. The eternal Son would have been fully himself in the unity of the Father and the Spirit even if, counterfactually, he had not freely come down and been incarnate and become human. In fact, the eternal Son would have been fully himself in the Trinity even if, counterfactually, the world itself had not been created. And that is why the Nicene Creed introduces this statement about creation at precisely this point in the creed, before entering into the gospel story: all things were made through him, and he came down. Placing the reference to creation at this point means double-underlining the fact that in taking on human nature, the Son was crossing over the line between Creator and creature without blurring or dissolving it. In terms of the development of Christian thought, the church did not enter the fourth century with a clearly expressed doctrine of what creation was and then ask which side of the line the Son was on. It was rather the case that confessing the Son's identity is what led Christian theology to become urgently, increasingly clear about affirming creation from nothing. A sharpened doctrine of creation was necessary to help shore up this christological distinction. A major function of the explicit Christian confession of creation is to clarify the articulation of the Son's identity.

This deep trinitarian background is the main way that the Nicene Creed takes a further step than the Apostles' Creed. What does this deep background have to do with union with Christ? This Nicene perspective on the gospel story makes two very important contributions to the doctrine of union with Christ. First, as we have seen, it deepens the personal identity of the Son. He is who he is because of how he is related to the Father, and that means that his identity is infinitely, omnipotently, eternally itself. Far from being contingent on the outcome of any history, the identity of the Son is as necessary as the reality of God. He truly comes among us and is present from the infinite depths of absolute perfection and fullness. This first function is a great grounding for union with Christ as something truly soteriological: the one who saves is God the Son. It is easy to see why the theologians who formulated and defended the Nicene theology believed they were faithfully restating the old faith in salvation by union with Christ but enriching that faith by specifying its eternal background.

But the second contribution made by the Nicene perspective on the gospel story is encapsulated in the formula "for us and for our salvation." It draws out the fact that everything that takes place below the Nicene line running between *theologia* and *oikonomia* is always already designed by God to be applied to us. That is, we go into the gospel story having been given reassurances in advance, from the doctrine of the Trinity and the doctrine of creation, that what the Son does in the incarnation he does for us. We do not hear the story first and then wait, wondering about what its application to us might be. That gap or interval between the work of Christ for us and the work of the Spirit applying it to us is not a gap of suspense. It is certainly not the case that, in the Jesus story, something happens that is irrelevant to us and that it is subsequently made relevant by the work of the Spirit applying it to us. That is not how application works. What the Nicene approach sheds light on is the fact that union with Christ in its broadest sense is functioning normatively both in the accomplishment of redemption and in the application of redemption. Later on we will see the reasons why it is valuable to talk about union with Christ in a more restricted sense, and to say why it especially belongs to the application side of the ledger under the work of the Spirit. But "especially" doesn't mean "exclusively." The incarnation is also already, in itself, for us and for our salvation. Union with Christ is too expansive (or in the words of John Murray, "broad and embracive")[10] to be contained under the heading of application.

By looking at the Apostles' and Nicene Creeds, we have briefly surveyed the status of union with Christ in early Christian thought. We have found both creeds to be documents that enshrine this doctrine by summarizing the life of Christ and setting it against an eternal background in the life of God. What we have seen is not quite enough to refute J. N. D. Kelly when he warns that any student studying "the soteriology of the fourth and early fifth centuries will be sharply disappointed if he expects to find anything corresponding to the elaborately worked out syntheses which the contemporary

10. Murray, *Redemption Accomplished and Applied*, 161.

theology of the Trinity and the Incarnation presents."[11] For one thing, there is nothing "elaborately worked out" in a short document like a creed; in that sense, we cannot really discern the full lineaments of christological and trinitarian thought here either. But union with Christ is obviously here, and centrally so. In the case of the Apostles' Creed, union with Christ is more prominent than the doctrine of the Trinity is. So it simply won't do to keep saying that the early church developed a Christology but not a soteriology.

But a lot of people do talk that way, and it is worth understanding why. One way of strengthening Kelly's case is to note the grain of truth in his observation that the early church did in fact hold councils on Trinity and Christology but not on redemption and soteriology. But even that observation needs to be sifted rather carefully. A careful study of the earliest ecumenical councils would show that the logic of union with Christ was in fact a driving factor behind most of the councils. Salvation was always at stake. In fact, while the topic of the councils was the nature of Christ, nevertheless the decisions were always animated by a soteriological concern, and not just implicitly or anonymously. In fact, the ecumenical councils stated more or less explicitly a number of principles that can be called soteriological axioms: Only God can save us (soteriology), so the savior must be God (Christology). What is not assumed is not healed (soteriology), so the savior must be fully human (Christology).[12] These principles, taken together, ought to be read as an expression of the theology of union with Christ elaborated in terms of its objective basis: as Christ's union with us that takes up into itself our union with Christ.

Conclusion

From this vantage point, the whole field of Christian theological history lies open before us, and I believe we could easily call dozens

11. Kelly, *Early Christian Doctrines*, 375.
12. I have traced this soteriological impulse in Sanders, "Biblical Grounding for the Christology of the Councils." See also O'Byrne, *"For Us and for Our Salvation."*

of witnesses from well-known classic writings and confessions in support of the claim that there is one Christian doctrine of salvation. It is the powerful, scriptural, spiritual drive toward union with Christ that gave rise to the creeds themselves and that flows out into faithful expositors of that creedal and credible "mere Christian" account of salvation. Of course there are differences and disagreements among various Christian traditions about important details within that soteriology, but in our day Christian disunity is often strategically exaggerated in a way that undercuts the clarity of the Christian message. We don't need to speculate about who benefits most immediately from Christian disunity. But we do need to strive to discern, wherever possible, the real unity we have. In chapter 3 we will call John Calvin as a key witness to the soteriology of union with Christ. Calvin was of course famously and conspicuously Protestant and stood opposed to Roman Catholic errors. But in soteriology, he consistently drew the main force of reformation from one clear source: the great Christian soteriology of union with Christ. We should do likewise and not be tricked by the spirit of the age into exaggerating Christian theological fragmentation.

I would like to close with a few suggestions for thinking and speaking rightly about salvation under this great rubric of union with Christ. While we shouldn't place much value in simply policing our language or correcting our habits of speech, we can start there and follow through with theological forms that match our corrected speech.

First, following this analysis of the creedal matrix of union with Christ, we should remember to speak of the one Christian doctrine of salvation, a single shared soteriology, and avoid pluralizing and multiplying soteriologies. We should not speak much of atonement theories, for reasons we will examine in greater detail in chapter 4. To argue well and fight fair about the doctrine of salvation, we should first invoke the overarching commonalities and then descend to the crucial details at a more local, specified level. When we do occasionally indulge in large-scale comparative soteriology, or contrasting certain aspects of atonement theology, we should take care that we are making wise use of these contrastive strategies rather than foolishly allowing ourselves to be used by them. Habits of Christian disunity are hard to break.

Second, once we are alert to the creedal matrix of union with Christ, we should continually touch base with this classic guidance about salvation by union with Christ. There is such a thing as theological progress, and things can get better, but the way forward for us in an ungrateful and forgetful epoch is certain to involve backing up and getting a running start from the deep history of the classic Christian tradition.

Third, moving in the other direction, we should gather all the wisdom we can from the ancient core confession of salvation by union with Christ, looking for ways to retrieve it and bring it forward for contemporary use. Our modern ways of handling soteriology are in many cases badly distorted by the decadent patterns of our theological and institutional cultures. We cannot simply go back to the classical modes, but we can retrieve and employ as much of them as we are able to understand.

Fourth, one thing we should retrieve is a kind of Christ-centeredness that is oddly alien to us, and thus difficult to retain. The classic creedal-patristic articulation of union with Christ was so wrapped up in tracing the identity of Jesus and narrating his work that the conventional wisdom of our age sometimes fails to recognize it as soteriology at all. It was so baked into the creedal matrix that we are in danger of thinking they were talking about not union with Christ but just Christ himself. We can learn from something here: a doctrine of union with Christ should rivet our attention on Jesus Christ. Asked in terms of a research program, How can a doctrine of union with Christ rivet our attention on Jesus Christ?

Fifth, a word from John Webster about the task of theology. In a 2002 autobiographical essay, Webster looked back on his rather defective training and made this resolution: "I resolved to structure the content of my teaching in accordance with the intellectual and spiritual logic of the Christian confession as it finds expression in the classical creeds, to allow that structure to stand and to explicate itself, and not to press the material into some other format."[13] He went on to name two tasks that followed from resolving to pursue theology in this manner:

> One is that of becoming acquainted with the history of Christian theology, and coming to understand it as the history of the church: as spiritual history, as a history of attempts to articulate the Gospel, and not just as a lumber room full of opinions to be submitted to the critical scrutiny of "valuers" and then auctioned off or discarded. The other task is that of trying to understand and think through the categories of classical dogmatics in their totality and their interrelations—to acquire a proper grasp of the architecture of dogmatics and to see its shape as the science of the Church's confession.[14]

In the matter of union with Christ, this seems to me to be the way of wisdom: "not to press the material into some other format" but to seek insight into how it explicates itself. As we have seen from our creedal study, the structure of Christian faith is itself a form of union with Christ; its first movement is rapt attention to Christ himself and its second movement is inclusion in him. In our next chapter we will trace that same structure in the forms of biblical revelation itself. The remaining chapters are attempts to let the material of union with Christ explicate itself in the form of our own theological thinking and our doxology.

13. Webster, "Discovering Dogmatics," 130–31.
14. Webster, "Discovering Dogmatics," 133.

DOXOLOGICAL INTERLUDE

Ephesians 2:4–7

But God, being rich in mercy, because of the great love with which he loved us, even when we were dead in our trespasses, made us alive together with Christ—by grace you have been saved—and raised us up with him and seated us with him in the heavenly places in Christ Jesus, so that in the coming ages he might show the immeasurable riches of his grace in kindness toward us in Christ Jesus.

CHAPTER TWO

Scripture in Christ

OF COURSE IT'S ALL IN PAUL. The most obvious way to begin studying the doctrine of union with Christ is to open your Bible to one of the key passages in which the apostle Paul writes about it. Among the many options, one of the richest veins to start mining would be the long argument in Romans 5 and 6, which raises all the right questions about union with Christ in just the right order and even answers most of them. Another promising place for prospectors would be Romans 8, where no digging is even necessary—the nuggets of gold are just scattered across the ground in plain sight. Finally, and most powerfully, Ephesians 2 draws believers into the vivifying, raising up, and enthronement of the Son. It is a particularly vivid and far-reaching statement on union with Christ, a "seat of doctrine" or principal text from which to teach. Union with Christ is, after all, a characteristically Pauline doctrine in numerous ways.

Indeed, anyone who writes at length about union with Christ is likely to begin wondering if all their work basically amounts to saying, in many words, what Paul sums up so concisely in two little words, a preposition and a name: "in Christ." In one sense, we can happily admit that everything we have to say about union with Christ never gets beyond that phrase. But as Kevin Vanhoozer reminds us, "There

29

is much room in the 'in' of 'in Christ.'"[1] That Vanhoozerian pun on the nativity at Bethlehem is significant. It leverages the language of Paul to point our attention to the life of Jesus. Paul, of course, would not be upset to have his language requisitioned in this way, because the logical structure of union with Christ begins with Jesus Christ and then moves to inclusion or incorporation into him. In canonical shorthand, we can say, "Gospel first, then epistle."[2] That sequence ought to make itself present somehow in the doctrine of union with Christ; we should find a way to put the Gospels-then-epistles logic to work in the systematic form of the doctrine.

In this chapter, we investigate the doctrine of union with Christ by attending to the genres in which it is primally and permanently expressed in Scripture. All Scripture is inspired; in fact, it is inspired on more levels and in more registers than we often note. Conservative evangelical bibliology is used to arguing for plenary verbal inspiration, with an emphasis on verbal: not just the ideas but the very words of this complex text are set in place by the divine author. By probing these genres, we intend to dig deeper into the "plenary" side of the equation and claim that not only the words but also the linguistic presuppositions and penumbrae gathered around those words—the grammatical categories, the patterns of meaning-making, and even the genres—were breathed out by the Holy Spirit.

What would it mean to affirm that the inspired words of Scripture come to us by way of inspired genres? Vanhoozer again: "Genre is not simply a device for classifying forms of literature, but a cognitive tool for generating worldviews."[3] In chapter 1 we looked at how the soteriology of union with Christ generated the creedal contours of early Christian confession; the soteriology gave both content and

---

1. Vanhoozer, "From 'Blessed in Christ' to 'Being in Christ,'" 10.

2. I call it shorthand because it skips over the fact that the earliest New Testament epistles were written before the canonical Gospels in their final form. To say the Gospels come first is to prioritize not their composition but their content: first the ministry of Jesus, then the ministry of Paul.

3. Vanhoozer, *Is There a Meaning in This Text?*, 343. See also Vanhoozer's earlier "Semantics of Biblical Literature"; and Abernethy, "Genre and Theological Vision."

Scripture in Christ

form to the creeds. In this chapter, we examine how that same soteriology generated the genre of Gospel and epistle in their Christian, canonical particularity. So first we will look at the genre of a Gospel and its theological significance for union with Christ. Second, we will look at the genre of apostolic epistle as a secondary literary type, whose argumentative structure is best apprehended as offering a supportive account of the significance of the life manifested in the Gospels. To frame it this way is to flip the ordinary expectation that union with Christ has a primarily Pauline foundation. But it coheres with the overall argument of this book that union with Christ is best recognized in a movement of thought that focuses primarily on Jesus Christ himself, and then connects believers to that one in whom is salvation.

The Genre of Gospel

Everybody knows what a Gospel is and that there are four real ones. A Gospel is a biography of Jesus, of course. But even though this answer may help you pick out a Gospel quickly across a crowded room, it is nevertheless not satisfying, least of all in the crowded room of New Testament studies. All the ways the Gospels behave somewhat like a biography pale in comparison to all the ways the Gospels *misbehave* by that standard. There are also problems of proportion and selectivity: Why would a Gospel like Mark, with only sixteen chapters to cover everything, devote six of those chapters to the final week of the main character's life? This apparent imbalance is what led Martin Kähler to offer, when speaking of Mark, what we might call a first proposed genre definition for Gospel:

> Genre Definition 1: A Gospel is a passion narrative with an extended introduction.[4]

---

4. Martin Kähler acknowledges that this is "to state the matter somewhat provocatively" (Kähler, *So-Called Historical Jesus and the Historic, Biblical Christ*, 80).

The balance and proportion that would make sense for narrating a thirty-three-year life, or even a three-year ministry, are distorted in the genre of Gospel by the subject matter itself. The sheer importance of what Jesus did and what was done to him in that final week reshapes biography from within and impresses on it the form of a passion narrative. Mark is not alone in giving such attention to the final week; Luke gives six of his twenty-four chapters to the final week and arranges another eight chapters around the dramatic progression to Jerusalem, where those events will take place. And Matthew, even with his large blocks of teaching that impressively round out the sense of Jesus's ministry as a teaching event, still assigns eight chapters out of his total twenty-eight chapters to the Passion Week. With just a bit of exaggeration, we could say these are more nearly death stories than life stories. At least we could say they are life stories uniquely leading up to death stories.

But consider a further specification. Moving beyond Kähler's definition, we can be more specific about how Gospels situate the life and death of Jesus:

> Genre Definition 2: A Gospel is a post-resurrection document of a pre-resurrection encounter.

A Gospel is the story of a resurrected person, written after the resurrection by an author who understands the meaning of the resurrection but is largely occupied with giving a sense of what it was like to be with that risen person before the resurrection, initially with no real understanding of the coming resurrection. A Gospel is a post-Easter document of a pre-Easter life. But the post-Easter understanding is baked into the telling of pre-Easter. The Gospels are written as proclamation in order, as John explicitly says, "that you may believe" (John 20:31). And each Gospel, in its own way, shares what it was like to make the transition from unbelief to belief: Mark with its messianic secret, John with its beautiful ironies, Luke-Acts with its hinge point of Pentecostal transformation, and Matthew with

Scripture in Christ

its multilayered discourses to be interpreted differently at different stages of reception. Each one leads the reader through pre-Easter perplexity to post-Easter perspicuity. The qualifications for being a Gospel author include the ability to mingle obscurity with clarity in the telling of the story, producing a text that can draw its readers along on the journey of faith. From this angle, the implied reader of a Gospel is somebody who is being led by the narrating master to understand the identity and significance of the narrated master.

Taken together, our first genre definition of a Gospel yields Christ crucified, and our second yields Christ risen. Affirming the centrality of both for a Gospel to be what it is, we can take them up into a third proposed definition:

> Genre Definition 3: A Gospel is a life of Christ, written in his presence.

We could expand the definition by saying "a life of the crucified and risen Christ," but we can take that as established; what we want to emphasize is it being written in his presence. Jesus, the subject of the Gospels, is truly alive and spiritually present to the writer of the Gospel; this reality exerts a peculiar pressure on the crafting of the Gospel genre itself. This is a more direct and personal way of describing what it means for a Gospel to be something written after the resurrection. It is not just the case that the author of a Gospel is conscious that the Jesus whose life moved toward death by crucifixion has gone on to vanish from the grave and move on somehow. That rising from the grave has had an effect on the Gospel author, who writes a document fully charged with the truth that Jesus Christ is alive. But the author of a Gospel does not write directly about his current encounter with the risen Jesus, narrating, for example, how he has come to know Jesus Christ in the power of the Holy Spirit in the midst of his own life and times as a believer; a Gospel is not a kind of personal conversion story describing the spiritual life of the writer.

Instead, what is key to the genre of Gospel is that its author writes a narrative precisely about the events of the life of Jesus leading toward that holy week; a narrative paying close attention to that holy week and recording what Jesus did and said on the pre-Easter side of the timeline. What we need to call to mind here is what the author of a Gospel has nothing to say about: his own personal testimony of his Christian experience, a life story about himself and his encounter with the post-resurrection Christ. No such story is given; instead, what is given is the story of Jesus. Gospels exist because the risen Christ oversees this kind of remembering of his life.

"His life on earth rose with him," in the words of nineteenth-century Anglican preacher Henry Scott Holland.[5] When Jesus rose from the dead, he not only came back to life but also brought back with him the life that he had already lived. In addition to being physically raised, he was also, we might say, biographically raised. His biography came to life with him and manifested its identity as the human life of a divine person. That biography is where we look to know him as he is; the medium of a personal encounter with Jesus here and now is the recounting of what he did and said then and there. The writing of a Gospel is empowered by the Holy Spirit, as we are used to confessing in our doctrine of Scripture, but it is also guided and shaped by the presence of the living one whose story is told in it. The living presence makes a crucial difference in what is selected and how it is narrated, because the words of a Gospel are the self-presentation of the risen Christ. John Henry Newman describes the spiritual dynamic underlying all Christian theological understanding in these words: "Though the Christian mind reasons out a series of dogmatic statements, one from another, this it has ever done, and always must do, not from those statements taken in themselves, as logical propositions, but as illustrated and (as I may say) inhabited by that sacred impression which is prior to them, which acts as a regulating principle, ever present, upon the reasoning, and without which

5. Holland, "Criticism and the Resurrection," 12.

Scripture in Christ

35

no one has any warrant to reason at all."[6] This is singularly the case in the production of the texts in the genre of canonical Gospel; its writers are "inhabited by that sacred impression" himself, "ever present."

In the classroom, I often illustrate this element in the Gospels by contrasting it with other life stories that are admirable and significant in themselves. Consider, for example, the life of Frederick Douglass (1818–95), or rather, his *lives*. Douglass was born into slavery, became educated and liberated, and worked for the education and liberation of his people. He wrote his own story three times: first, in the classic *Narrative of the Life of Frederick Douglass, an American Slave* (1845); then at greater length in *My Bondage and My Freedom* (1855); and finally at much greater length and with several more decades of experience to narrate in *Life and Times of Frederick Douglass* (1893).[7] There are some genre similarities with the Gospels here. Douglass's three books go back over the same material, creating various kinds of synoptic problems as he tells some of the same stories from different angles and with different details. But the main formal similarity to the Gospels is the time sequence. In the case of Douglass, writing from the far, safe side of freedom and literacy, he tells the story of what it was like to be enslaved and illiterate and how things went when he was in that state. Event after event in the life of the young Douglass is faithfully and accurately narrated but always suffused with the adult literary intelligence of an emancipated, empowered, and well-traveled author. These similarities to the Gospel genre are helpful for drawing out the dynamics of Gospel narration. But of course the differences are equally striking: Frederick Douglass wrote autobiographically, whereas Gospel writers wrote about somebody else. And Douglass wrote, we might say, in his own presence, whereas Gospel writers wrote in the presence of another.

But the real difference, the infinite qualitative distinction between the life of Frederick Douglass and the life of Jesus Christ, comes into

6. Newman, *Sermons*, 335–36.
7. All three are in Gates, *Frederick Douglass*.

play when we consider not the Gospel writer but the Gospel reader. Let us bring this out by proposing another definition of Gospel:

> Genre Definition 4: A Gospel is a life of Christ, written in his presence, to be read in his presence.

When we read the life, or the lives, of Frederick Douglass, we read them as artifacts of an absent author. Frederick Douglass lived, wrote his own life, and died. He recedes now into our national past, and if we say we know him personally, we are describing only the literary reenactment of a historical process now slipping further into the past. "Time like an ever-rolling stream bears all its sons away."[8] If we say Frederick Douglass lives on, we mean it in a metaphorical sense, referring to the impact his life has made on our national history. If we were to try to take too seriously the claim that Douglass lives, we would only make his absence more conspicuous. If we started a society that met once a week for the public reading of his life story, and gathered to sing songs about him, and called our society after his name, we would only be making it obvious that no merely human life can support the kind of religious devotion underwritten by the Gospels. It would become increasingly sad; the more we tried to conjure up an ongoing presence that was more than literary or historical remembrance, the more we would underline the fact that Douglass is no longer with us.

By contrast, when reading a Gospel, "he whose biography is now before us, is himself with us." This principle is explained and applied by Scottish theologian Hugh Martin (1822–85) in his 1860 book *Christ's Presence in the Gospel Narrative* (republished under the title *The Abiding Presence*).[9] The key idea Martin develops is that we have

---

8. Isaac Watts, "O God Our Help in Ages Past."

9. I will be citing Martin, *Abiding Presence*. The original publication was *Christ's Presence in the Gospel Narrative* (London: T. Nelson and Sons, 1860). "He whose biography is now before us, is himself with us" is from p. 16. I have written about this aspect of Martin's work at https://scriptoriumdaily.com/the-biography-and-the-presence/.

two factors to reckon with when we read the life of Christ in Scripture: first, the biography set down in print ("before us"); and second, the living presence of the risen Christ ("with us").

Martin sets out to "ponder . . . the marvellous advantage of possessing this presence and biography unitedly."[10] He shows the value of their unity by imagining them separately: What if we only had one or the other?

> If all we had was a written biography of Jesus, we would use it as a way of recalling his amazing life that took place long ago, and that life would get further away from us with every passing year. "Oh! Would that I had been there!" One fears that this is what many believers are in danger of settling for: a life of Jesus that is not much more than a life of Lincoln or of Napoleon.[11]

Or, we might add, of Douglass. Conversely, if all we had was the presence of the risen Christ, but no written biography, what would we have? A powerful spiritual reality, Christ himself. But what would our thoughts and conceptions of that presence be? What would guide them or shape them? "All is vague and hazy, very solemnizing . . . very encouraging and consoling; but very indefinite also, and withal, somewhat ghostly."[12] Before long, instead of concrete knowledge of the life of Jesus Christ, our minds and affections would fill up with "emotions, imaginations, and conceptions" of our own provision; "mere pietistic, sentimental conceptions of his presence, and . . . perhaps fanatical emotions begotten of the belief that he is present with me."[13] One fears that this is what many believers are in danger of settling for: an unformed and undisciplined sense of Christ's presence, always shading off into a personal Jesus shaped to fit our own heads or hearts.

10. Martin, *Abiding Presence*, 16.
11. Martin, *Abiding Presence*, 17.
12. Martin, *Abiding Presence*, 18.
13. Martin, *Abiding Presence*, 18.

With his sure and spiritual presence, then, let it be my privilege to possess his clear and definite biography. Give me the presence of the Lord—not vague, indistinct, and ghostly; silent, oppressive, and almost appalling—but as uttering the very sayings, and achieving the very works of grace and love that the biography details. Let me hear this Saviour, present with me, saying (as in this history) to Peter and James and John, "What I say to you I say to all," so that I am entitled to hear it as said to me. Let the ever-present Christ make his presence with me definite, intelligible, and most distinct, by proffering to me—as still full of spirit and life, of grace and glory—the very words he uttered and the works he did in the days of his flesh. Let him enshrine his promised presence within the very lineaments and limits of the biography.[14]

To have both the presence of the ascended Christ and the inspired written account of his earthly life is to have something true and to know Christ. "The presence gives reality, present reality, and life, to the biography: the biography supplies to the otherwise indefinite presence distinct manifestation, action, and utterance."[15] More concisely, "the biography is enlivened by the presence: the presence is defined by the biography." And Martin concludes his opening chapter with the wish "Let the biography and the presence be conjoined and coalesce."[16]

Both senses, biography and presence, are contained, for those who have ears to hear, in the phrase "the life of Jesus." We might call a book about anybody their "life." And in another sense we might equally call anybody's living presence a "life." But readers who encounter the reality of Christ himself in the act of reading the Gospels have both factors at work: the life and the life, the biography and the presence.

It is obvious enough that faith in Christ gave rise to written accounts of his life and teachings. But these written accounts are unlike

14. Martin, *Abiding Presence*, 19.
15. Martin, *Abiding Presence*, 20.
16. Martin, *Abiding Presence*, 20.

Scripture in Christ

conventional lives in ways that are theologically significant. They are meant to be read in the presence of their subject, in such a way that the historical account and the actual spiritual presence of the risen Christ converge on the reader (both the implied reader and the actual reader). Gospels, in other words, are not inert genres; they do not sit still and await application. They are instead the primal and inescapable literary form of the self-presentation of the risen Christ. They are in themselves already documents of union with Christ, and the implied reader is a disciple united to Christ's life by faith.

Apostolic Epistles as Interpretive Guides

To complete the sequence of "Gospel first, then epistle," we turn to the epistles—that is, we turn to the genre of New Testament writing that is made up of letters from apostles. These documents, especially the ones by Paul, are where the theology of union with Christ is articulated in its most explicit doctrinal form. The argument of an epistle often has a narrative substructure, but just barely. Honesty compels us to admit that it is a substructure with a decided emphasis on the prefix "sub-." The outline of a narrative, either of Israel or of the life of Jesus, is not evident on the surface of most epistles.[17] Nevertheless, the story does lurk there beneath the argument. The Jesus story is just below the surface, guiding the theological arguments, and sometimes it breaks through and makes itself evident.

Raised with Christ in Ephesians

The classic place the life-of-Christ substructure of Paul's soteriology can be seen most conspicuously is in Ephesians 1 and 2, where Paul first describes what God did in the life of Christ himself and then explains how it applies to believers. That is, when Paul wants to describe salvation, he first tells what happened to Jesus and then

17. See the thorough discussion in Longenecker, *Narrative Dynamics in Paul*, especially Francis Watson's chapter, "Is There a Story in These Texts?" (231–40).

annexes believers to that happening. God demonstrated his saving power "in Christ when he raised him from the dead and seated him at his right hand in the heavenly places" (Eph. 1:20). The key verbs here are "raised" and "seated," describing the way God glorified Christ after the crucifixion. Then in Ephesians 2:5–6, as he turns to a description of the new life God has given to the church, Paul picks out those same mighty actions—raising, seating—and redeploys them: God "raised us up with him and seated us with him in the heavenly places in Christ Jesus." In fact, he uses a grammatical strategy for making the identification as direct as possible. He repeats the same verbs but adds an inclusive prefix to them. We are co-raised and co-seated with Christ (in Greek the actual prefix is *syn-*). What took place first in the life of Jesus is now somehow reenacted in faith by, or extended to, believers. That power that God exercised in Christ is also God's power "toward us who believe" (Eph. 1:19). It is not just a similar kind of power or a second discrete outflow from the same reservoir of power. God's power toward believers (1:19) is precisely the power by which he raised Christ himself from the dead (1:20). We can make some kind of distinction between them, of course. Christ is first, and we follow. We might say that the same divine exercise of power has its effects in two phases, working first in Christ and then in those who are included in him. That is chronologically true (current believers coming along at a distance of two millennia), but it is chiefly a matter of logical priority. What happens in Christ himself comes first; the structure of salvation is a work wrought in him, in which we are next included.

Once Paul has fully stated both moments of this saving power, the two moments can be compared:

Christ (Eph. 1:20)	Believers (Eph. 2:5–6)
Raised from the dead	Co-raised
Seated at God's right hand in the heavenly places	Co-seated in the heavenly places in him

Scripture in Christ

41

Believers are bundled into Christ such that their salvation results from the work God does in Christ. It would be misleading to say that Christ has his resurrection and we have ours; the soteriological point is that Christ's resurrection is ours. This is recognizably Paul's soteriology from numerous places in his letters.[18] The grammatical strategy of Ephesians 2:5–6 is to make this conspicuous by bundling us into Christ with a tight set of "co-" inclusions.

It would be enough simply to line up these two columns and trace the way a full understanding of Christ yields such a rich and integrated understanding of being in Christ. That would adequately unlock the "Gospel first, then epistle" structure of biblical soteriology. But there is more to see if we look deeper into the argument of Ephesians. Two things deserve closer attention here.

First, Paul supplies an extra verb on the believers' side of the ledger: "made alive." Where Christ was (1) raised and (2) seated, believers are said to be (1) made alive, (2) raised, and (3) seated. In fact, Paul not only starts his second sequence with the new verb but puts the prefix of inclusion (*syn-* in Greek) onto all three of these verbs, extending his "co-" strategy of showing our inclusion in what was done to Christ. It is a peculiar move, leaving more verbs in the derivative right column than were in the foundational left column:

Christ (Eph. 1:20)	Believers (Eph. 2:5–6)
	Co-made alive together with Christ
Raised from the dead	Co-raised
Seated at God's right hand in the heavenly places	Co-seated in the heavenly places in him

A reader might reasonably expect to be given the basic verb ("he made Christ alive") before being given the prefixed verb ("he co-made us alive together with Christ"). But Paul does not follow that predictable plan. He does not build a platform of "he made Christ

18. For a survey of Paul's usage that carefully accounts for the various ways Paul writes and the full range of terms he uses, see Campbell, *Paul and Union with Christ*.

alive" in the first place and then extend it to believers. We might of course discern an unstated "made alive" in the verb "raised from the dead." But while it is left implicit on the left, it first becomes explicit on the right. The argument of Ephesians introduces "made alive" as an explicit category only when believers' inclusion in the salvation accomplished in Christ is under consideration.

Second, Paul interrupts the second sequence of verbs by interjecting the statement "by grace you have been saved." So the tidy parallelism between Christ and believers, while still the dominant structure of the passage, is rendered lopsided by an unparalleled verb and then broken by an interjection:

Christ (Eph. 1:20)	Believers (Eph. 2:5–6)
	Co-made alive together with Christ
	—by grace you have been saved—
Raised from the dead	Co-raised
Seated at God's right hand in the heavenly places	Co-seated in the heavenly places

The interjection is a short, early occurrence of the longer formula Paul will deploy in verse 8. There he will not only say "by grace you have been saved" but go on to add "through faith. And this is not your own doing; it is the gift of God." Why give a short preview in verse 5 of the statement about grace that he will make much more fully in verse 8?

These two minor peculiarities of Ephesians 2 don't exactly demand a deep explanation. Plenty of fairly trivial reasons might account for phenomena like this. Paul could be introducing variety into his diction (an extra verb disrupting parallelism) or breaking up his discourse for purely rhythmic reasons (an interjected phrase). But if we are tracing the larger soteriological movement of thought from the life of Christ to the experience of the believer, we may take these peculiarities as clues to something deeper. At least one major interpreter has seen something profound lurking in the surprising turns of phrase in Ephesians 2:5–6. Thomas Goodwin (1600–1680) argues that Paul speaks the way he does because he has in mind two different phases or aspects of our participation in Christ. On the one hand is the experienced moment of spiritual conversion, a point in our own biographies in which God applies to us the work of Christ. This Paul calls being "made alive together with Christ." On the other hand, we are already included in Christ representatively in such a way that everything that has happened to him is ours in principle by virtue of our inclusion in it. This Paul calls being "raised up" and "seated in the heavenly places in Christ." On Goodwin's close reading of the passage, Paul "severs, as it were, quickening from being raised."[19] Why does Paul make a division here? He does so in order to mark the difference between the quickening we have already experienced "with Christ" in our own lives of faith and the resurrection and enthronement that are not yet aspects of our experience but truly belong to us in Christ. According to Goodwin, the interjection "by grace you have been saved" is there to mark this break between quickening and raising/seating, and it alerts the reader to the present possession of a state of salvation.

If Goodwin is right—and he admits that his method is to find as much depth in every word of the text as is possible—then Ephesians 2:5–6 presupposes a layered understanding of union with Christ. It includes the foundational or comprehensive layer of all that God the Father did for believers when he raised Christ from the dead, signified here by the conclusive realities of resurrection and enthronement. And it also includes the present experience of spiritual renewal, revival, awakening, or renovation, signified by "quickening" or "being made alive." As Goodwin says,

> When he [Paul] speaks of quickening, it is a work already done in us; as it was once done in Christ for us, so it has its accomplishment in a measure, therefore we are said to be quickened together in Christ, as

19. Goodwin, *Epistle to the Ephesians*, 235.

also with Christ; for that is a true rule, that those works which were done in Christ for us, after they are begun to be wrought in us, we are said to have them wrought in us together with Christ.[20]

If Paul's order of exposition in 2:1–10 were more systematic-theological, he would no doubt have stated the foundational union first: we are included in the past act of Christ's resurrection and being seated in the heavens. He would then have mentioned our current experience of awakening or enlivening. But in these first ten verses of Ephesians 2, he is following instead the story of our experience of salvation: first we were dead in trespasses and sins (2:1), but then we were made alive with Christ (2:5) so that finally "in the coming ages he might show the immeasurable riches of his grace in kindness toward us in Christ Jesus" (2:7). "The Apostle speaks to these Ephesians by way of application," as Goodwin notes.[21] In this order of exposition, it would make no sense to begin speaking about the spiritual truth of our being raised and seated in Christ until the experienced reality of being made alive together with him is introduced. And as we have seen, Paul did in fact already lay the foundation of our inclusion in Christ when, in chapter 1, he talked directly about what God did in the life of Christ himself. Even in telling that Jesus story in 1:20, Paul had in view the fact that God's power for the salvation of believers was at work "when he raised him from the dead and seated him at his right hand in the heavenly places."

In other words, what we have described as the "Gospel first, then epistle" structure of union with Christ is echoed here in the epistle itself. The payoff in Ephesians can be stated more briefly as the difference between salvation "in Christ" and salvation "together with" Christ. Again following Goodwin's lead, "in Christ" signifies the comprehensive reality of inclusion in him, but "with Christ" indicates the portion of that union that has already made the decisive difference in the experience of believers. Goodwin notes,

20. Goodwin, *Epistle to the Ephesians*, 235–36.
21. Goodwin, *Epistle to the Ephesians*, 240.

Scripture in Christ   45

You see the distinction between *in Christ* and *with Christ*. We are said to be quickened with Christ. Why? Because that work, as it is wrought in Christ once for us, hath now some accomplishment in us; but speaking of the resurrection to come, he doth not say we are raised up *with* Christ, but raised up *in* Christ. . . . Learn, I say, to distinguish between receiving a thing *in* Christ, and receiving it *with* Christ. You receive it with Christ when it is actually applied to your person.[22]

We have lingered over Ephesians because it famously makes such elaborate use of "in Christ" soteriology. It is the most conspicuous illustration of the New Testament's overall tendency to start with the Jesus story and then include believers within it. Thomas Goodwin's intense scrutiny of one key passage from Ephesians makes the point more conspicuous yet (even for readers who cannot join him in affirming such detailed distinctions). As we continue this chapter, we will indicate just a few ways in which the rest of the New Testament's epistolary witness manifests the same soteriological dynamic. The epistles are consistently oriented toward explaining how believers have salvation by inclusion in the Gospels; they teach about life in Christ.

The Other Pauline Epistles

A glance at Paul's other letters shows that the same theme of salvation "in Christ" is prominent in all his writings. Ephesians may be the most elaborate development of the theme, but it is a theme hardly understated in the rest of Paul.[23] Not only does Paul speak often

22. Goodwin, *Epistle to the Ephesians*, 246 (italics original). Goodwin uses the English prepositions "in" and "with" to make his theological point clear, but he is aware that "with" is represented in the Greek text of Eph. 2:5 by the dative case. I take it to be a dative of association, well represented in English by "with" and notably different from the "in Christ" formula of 2:6.

23. A book on union with Christ hardly needs any excuse for focusing on Ephesians, but perhaps some readers will have stumbled at the decision to appeal directly to this letter, whose authorship is disputed by modern scholarship, rather than to an epistle with undisputed Pauline authorship or to the principal letters (the *Hauptbriefe*). I do affirm Pauline authorship of Ephesians, but many who doubt or reject it on critical grounds nevertheless often

of dying and rising with or in[24] Christ, but he even uses the same grammatical device of joining believers to the Savior using prefixes of inclusion. Paul says of himself that he has been co-crucified with Christ (Gal. 2:20). He tells us that we are co-inheritors with Christ (Rom. 8:17).[25] We see that salvation pervades Paul's writings as the thing God did in Christ—and the life of faith as co-that. Again and again the good news includes the verbs of Jesus and the prefix that annexes our destiny to his.

Meanwhile in 1 Corinthians, Paul deploys the "in Christ" formula strategically to gather up all the blessings of salvation and locate them in one place. Consider the remarkable argument that God is the agent who locates us there, so that "because of him you are in Christ Jesus, who became to us wisdom from God, righteousness and sanctification and redemption, so that, as it is written, 'Let the one who boasts, boast in the Lord'" (1 Cor. 1:30–31). This is a strikingly compact statement of the one cause and the many results of salvation. The King James Version renders the first part even more concisely: "Of him are ye in Christ." But no sooner does Paul deploy this concentrated statement of union than he unfolds it into the full range of its manifold effects. How much there is for us in Christ: wisdom, righteousness, sanctification, redemption. Each of these four weighty words could be explored in great depth. In the tradition flowing from Calvin, special attention has been given to the way the two middle

---

acknowledge that it seems almost designed to serve as an introduction to Paul's main ideas, especially on this topic. F. F. Bruce often treated Ephesians as "the quintessence of Paulinism" in a way that transcended authorship questions. See Bruce, *Paul*, 424.

24. Goodwin did not offer his in-with distinction as a general guide to biblical usage; he used it to draw out the principles of Eph. 2. It should certainly not be pressed as some sort of rule.

25. Only for brevity's sake am I glossing over a significant difference between the "in Christ" motif in Ephesians and Colossians and in the rest of his letters. Typically Paul prefers to say that we have died with Christ (past tense) and we will rise with Christ (future tense). Ephesians and Colossians follow a different usage by including our rising and enthronement in the past tense with Christ's own. The difference has implications that richly repay closer study. For our purposes, it is enough to point out that Goodwin's in-with distinction is designed precisely to align Ephesians with Paul's way of writing elsewhere.

terms, "righteousness" (that is, "justification") and "sanctification," are comprehended under the single heading of union with Christ in these verses. Calvin himself, in a celebrated passage, writes of the benefits of union,

> Let us sum these up. Christ was given to us by God's generosity, to be grasped and possessed by us in faith. By partaking of him, we principally receive a double grace: namely, that being reconciled to God through Christ's blamelessness, we may have in heaven instead of a Judge a gracious Father; and secondly, that sanctified by Christ's spirit we may cultivate blamelessness and purity of life.[26]

The "double grace" points to the way two major aspects of Paul's soteriology, the forensic and the transformative, are integrated within the larger category of our union with Christ.[27]

For our purposes, it would be convenient if Paul were a bit more explicit in the immediate context of 1 Corinthians 1:30 about how all four of these blessings of salvation are established first in the life of Jesus Christ and then take place in us when God places us in Christ. An exposition of the life of Christ instantiating wisdom, righteousness, sanctification, and redemption simply does not fit the flow of Paul's discourse in the opening of 1 Corinthians. But much of that content could be fetched from the narratives invoked later in the letter ("The Lord Jesus on the night when he was betrayed took bread, and when he had given thanks, he broke it" [11:23–24]) and from Paul's handing on the report that "Christ died for our sins in accordance with the Scriptures, that he was buried, that he was raised on the third day in accordance with the Scriptures" (15:3–4). What a rewarding study it would be to scan the Gospels for instances of Christ exhibiting divine wisdom, righteousness, sanctification, and

---

26. Calvin, *Institutes of the Christian Religion* III.11, 725.

27. There has emerged a vast controversial literature on the implications of this *duplex gratia* for Reformed soteriology. Instructive as the conflict is in its own context, it can be somewhat distracting. A helpful entry with a special focus on 1 Cor. 1:30 is Garcia, *Life in Christ*.

redemption throughout his ministry. The instinct to do so, I am suggesting, is in line with the basic intention of the New Testament epistle genre. The genre of the apostolic epistles is that of a secondary literary type that presupposes the realities set forth in the Gospels and brings in a supportive account of the significance of the life manifested there.

Outside the Pauline Epistles

There are more than these two genres in the New Testament, of course: there are New Testament apocalyptic and wisdom writings. And even within the genres of Gospel and epistle there are complex literary phenomena that need to be recognized using other literary descriptors. But the Spirit-driven genres of Gospel and epistle are the ones that most clearly manifest the structure of union with Christ not only in their explicit content but in their form.

Furthermore, even as we establish the contours of this Gospels-epistles distinction, we just as quickly must acknowledge the existence of the Johannine writings: the Gospel of John, the three Johannine epistles, and the Revelation. In this subset of texts, we hear a theological voice that speaks fluently not only in Gospel and epistle but also in that strangest of biblical genres: apocalypse.[28] But the genre-crossing Johannine performance does not invalidate the distinction. In fact, these documents underline the main point of our argument in their own distinctive way, because taken as a whole they articulate the soteriology of union with Christ in an especially powerful way. In a recent book, Clive Bowsher has traced the theme of union with Christ across the Fourth Gospel and the three Johannine epistles.[29] While he is careful to "avoid exegetical 'crosstalk' between the Gospel and epistles" in his initial survey of their messages, Bowsher

---

28. The literary similarities among these five "Johannine" documents are, I hope, adequate to make these observations satisfying even to critics who assign the texts to different sources.

29. Bowsher, *Life in the Son*. See also Bennema, "'Union with Christ' in the Johannine Writings."

traces such a similar soteriology of "Johannine 'in-one-anotherness' of believers and the Father-Son" in both sources that he is finally able to synthesize them.[30] In the Johannine texts of the New Testament, then, we have a single voice that performs both Gospel and epistle.

Taking a sufficiently broad view of this superstructure of "Gospel first, then epistle," we are also able to look back on the vast testimony of the Old Testament and acknowledge its importance. Just as epistles are secondary and supportive literary forms that necessarily follow the life of Jesus by explaining and applying it in another discursive form, the New Testament itself is a literary deposit that presupposes the Old Testament. The New Testament does more than simply explain and apply the Old Testament, of course. Between the writing of the literary documents of the two Testaments, an event has occurred in history: Christ himself has come, and in Christ God has not just added a new explanation but has actually brought about a great change. That change is the accomplishing in Christ of the salvation promised throughout the Old Testament. The Old Testament way of saying "in Christ" would be to speak of inclusion in the promised messiah as the fulfillment of all God's ways and works. From that perspective, the one unified witness of Scripture can be understood as the promise of inclusion in the Messiah, and the fulfillment of that promise as narrated in the Gospels and explained in the epistles. Paul implies as much when he says that "Christ died for our sins in accordance with the Scriptures" (1 Cor. 15:3). Here we have an epistle retelling a Gospel event on the basis of the Old Testament. We have made distinctions among the genres precisely to show how they work together rather than separately.

Conclusion

The coworking of the biblical genres reminds us that this "Gospel first, then epistle" schema is offered as a way of grasping how the

30. Bowsher, *Life in the Son*, 3–4.

soteriology of union with Christ is expressed in the literary form of the Scriptures. If we learn to recognize the spiritual structure of that soteriology—the two moments of salvation being worked out in Christ before believers are subsequently included in that salvation—then we can see the same theological structure present in the contours of the canon, in the deep structures of its literary forms. But when we use the shorthand "Gospel first, then epistle," we should not take these categories as exclusive rules about what can and cannot be found in the details of the documents. We should freely admit that sometimes an epistle includes a narrative component (recall 1 Corinthians' direct telling of how Christ served the supper and then died and rose again). And we should certainly recognize that the canonical Gospels do not consist of raw, uninterpreted biographical data points. These reports of the life of Christ are obviously proclamations of salvation in Christ (recall the supernatural character of our final definition of the genre of Gospel as "a life of Christ, written in his presence, to be read in his presence"). One benefit of gaining insight into the spiritual structure of inclusion in Christ is that it changes our posture toward the overall message of Scripture. Even while we continue to read the Bible to find its witness about union with Christ, we become aware that the Bible itself exists, in the very literary forms and genres in which it exists, because it is itself situated in Christ. Union with Christ is what summoned these particular genres of prophecy and promise, Gospel, and epistle.

DOXOLOGICAL INTERLUDE

Three Mysteries (Saphir)

Let us ever with adoring hearts believe in the three unions which the Church of Christ has confessed in all ages.

First, we behold Jesus, God and man, two natures in one Person; the Lord of Glory, Immanuel, God with us. Beholding Christ, God and man, we see the Father and receive the Spirit.

Thus we learn to adore, secondly, the eternal and essential union of Father, Son, and Holy Ghost. The Saviour reveals to us the eternal love of the Father; we know Christ as the Word by whom all things were made, as the Only-begotten, loved before the foundation of the world. We know Him also as the Heir, who shall inherit all things. Accepted in the Beloved, and seated with Him in the heavenly places, we adore the love of the Father who chose us in Christ, and look forward to the glory which the heirs of God and the joint-heirs with the Son shall possess. And we know and adore also the Holy Ghost, one with the Father and the Son in eternity, in creation, and in redemption, by whose power and gracious indwelling the Father's love and the Saviour's grace are revealed and communicated to our souls unto eternal life.

We believe also, thirdly, the union, which, according to the will of the Father, subsists between Christ and the Church. Of God are we in Christ: the Father is the Husbandman, the Son incarnate is the Vine, we who believe are the branches. The Father is supreme Lord and King, the Son incarnate is the Bridegroom, and we who trust in Him and love Him are the bride. We are members of the Body of which Christ is the

Head; and the Head of Christ is God. By the Holy Ghost Christ and the Church are one; He is in them, and they are inseparable from Him in life and death, in time and eternity.

We believe these unions, though we cannot comprehend and fathom them. We have a knowledge and experience of these mysteries in our hearts and lives, an assurance and consolation continually flowing from these eternal depths, and we wait with calmness and hope for the bright and perfect knowledge which shall be ours when we see face to face. Eternity alone can unfold the blessedness of those who know "the name of the Father, and of the Son, and of the Holy Ghost."[1]

1. Saphir, *Christ and the Church*, 87–88.

CHAPTER THREE

Variations on a Soteriological Theme

THE MAJOR BURDENS OF OUR ARGUMENT have been (1) that there is such a thing as one central Christian view of salvation and (2) that union with Christ is it. Just as C. S. Lewis celebrated the spacious and plentiful reality of "mere Christianity," we can in perfectly good conscience affirm that union with Christ is the church's "mere soteriology." To overlook the massiveness, solidity, and centrality of this soteriological theme is dangerous, because to look past it is to doom ourselves to searching for some other answer. If we intend to keep union with Christ steadily in view, we may need to unlearn a number of distracting bad habits in our ways of perceiving and describing salvation. Nevertheless, there is real diversity in the way the theme of union with Christ is developed and elaborated by various confessions and traditions. Indeed, if this core soteriology is as broad and inclusive as we are arguing, we would expect it to take on local color and flavor from the multiple theological and spiritual cultures and subcultures in which it is expressed. Some of the resulting variety is just a matter of regional differences, shifts of emphasis, or enculturated patterns of inflection. But some of the variety rises to the level of actual doctrinal disagreement. In this chapter, we will survey a range

53

of variations on the central soteriological theme of union with Christ. There is even a variety of varieties and different kinds of differences; we will look at differences of structure, weight, and genre.

John Calvin and the Creedal Setting of Union with Christ

In order to reconnect with the creedal setting of union with Christ traced in chapter 1, we cannot do better than turn to a classic statement by John Calvin. Rarely has the creedal centrality of union been put into play as well as in Calvin's placement of it in the *Institutes*. The classic location is *Institutes* book II, chapter 16. In book II, Calvin works through the life of Christ, following roughly the order of the Apostles' Creed, which he says he has followed "because it states the leading articles of redemption in a few words, and may thus serve as a tablet in which the points of Christian doctrine, most deserving of attention, are brought separately and distinctly before us."[1] Then, after having analyzed how each aspect of Christ's work is effective for us and our salvation, Calvin delivers this comprehensive summary:

> We see that our whole salvation and all its parts are comprehended in Christ. We should therefore take care not to derive the least portion of it from anywhere else. If we seek salvation, we are taught by the very name of Jesus that it is "of him." If we seek any other gifts of the Spirit, they will be found in his anointing. If we seek strength, it lies in his dominion; if purity, in his conception; if gentleness, it appears in his birth. For by his birth he was made like us in all respects that he might learn to feel our pain. If we seek redemption, it lies in his passion; if acquittal, in his condemnation; if remission of the curse, in his cross; if satisfaction, in his sacrifice; if purification, in his blood; if reconciliation, in his descent into hell; if mortification of the flesh, in his tomb; if newness of life, in his resurrection; if immortality, in the same; if inheritance of all blessings, in his Kingdom; if untroubled expectation of judgment, in the power given to him to judge. In short,

1. Calvin, *Institutes of the Christian Religion* II.16.18, 527.

since rich store of every kind of good abounds in him, let us drink our fill from this fountain, and from no other.[2]

Alert readers notice that Calvin is rehearsing the Gospel story of Jesus, but specifically in the terms of the Apostles' Creed: cross, descent into hell, resurrection. It is the story of Jesus, but specifically in the concise narration of the creed. What Calvin is doing in these elaborate sentences is taking the points of the creed and drawing out their soteriological implications. Each of these actions of Christ has saving power, and Calvin names each of them in turn with his if-then structure: if we seek redemption, then it is found in the passion; if we seek eternal life, then it is to be found in his resurrection; and so on.

His long sentences of many "ifs" are sandwiched between shorter ones that make two related points about the comprehensiveness and exclusivity of the salvation that is found in Christ: It is not just some of our salvation, or parts of it, but "our whole salvation and all its parts" that are in Christ, as "a rich store of every kind of good." Therefore we must "take care not to derive the least portion of it from anywhere else," but to "drink our fill from this fountain, and from no other." It is all in Christ, and you should seek no other, Calvin insists. Calvin was of course in the business of reforming; he was preaching into a church culture that was trying to find its way out of a settled pattern of supplementing salvation with a little of this, that, and the other thing. Salvation in Christ is comprehensive and complete, utterly shutting out other saviors. This reformational conclusion depends on Calvin making his case in the central sentences, drawing water joyfully from the well of salvation by returning over and over, "if" after "if," to the things confessed in the middle of the Apostles' Creed.

Calvin's close following of the Apostles' Creed is even more evident if we consider what he has done with the creed's recitation of the titles "Jesus," "Christ," and "Lord." He employs these three christological

2. Calvin, *Institutes of the Christian Religion* II.16.19, 527–28.

titles powerfully, but they may be somewhat obscured by the way Calvin works back and forth among their Hebrew and Greek origins. From the name "Jesus" he takes the notion of salvation, since the name is derived from the Hebrew words for "YHWH is salvation." From the title "Christ" Calvin takes the notion of receiving the Holy Spirit, since the title refers to one who is anointed ("messiah" from Hebrew, "Christ" from Greek). The presence of the title "Lord" in Calvin's sentence is perhaps the most subtle, but it is more evident if you compare the creed in Latin to what Calvin wrote in his Latin *Institutes*. He says, "If we seek strength, it lies in his dominion." The reason Calvin talks about dominion here is that it is answering to the creed's confession that Jesus Christ is Lord—that is, *Dominus* in Latin. We have strength from him being *Dominus*, having dominion. So the creed's string of christological titles (Jesus, Christ, Lord) all show up in Calvin as:

Jesus (that is, YHWH is salvation): "If we seek salvation, we are taught by the very name of Jesus."
Christ (that is, the anointed one): "If we seek any other gifts of the Spirit, they will be found in his anointing."
Lord (that is, *Dominus*): "If we seek strength, it lies in his dominion."

After he unpacks all that is compressed in the titles of "Lord," "Jesus," and "Christ," the rest of the creedal structure is much more obvious. He explicitly follows the narrative sequence: conception, birth, passion, condemnation, cross, and so on, all the way to our "untroubled expectation of judgment" based on his coming "to judge" the living and the dead. It is a masterful, even delightful, interaction with the creed's soteriology. It is the doctrine of union with Christ displayed in its creedal form, functioning at the hinge point of Calvin's developed soteriology.

Having already drawn attention to some of its beauties that are in danger of being lost in translation, we can similarly note that Calvin's

Reformation polemic against Roman Catholic errors and distortions would have been more evident to sixteenth-century readers of ecclesiastical Latin. Several of the benefits of union with Christ that Calvin enumerates were key words in the medieval Roman Catholic pastoral care system: gentleness/indulgence (*indulgentia*), absolution (*absolutio*), remission of sins (*remissio*), satisfaction (*satisfactio*), and purgation (*purgatio*). Though the words are very similar in English, it is easy to miss what this careful word choice was accomplishing for sixteenth-century readers. As Calvin moves through the creed's sequence of the benefits of union with Christ, he uses them to answer the long list of our spiritual needs, and by doing so he shows how the sacramental-ecclesial mediatorial system of the Roman Catholic Church had been displaced in advance by the sufficiency of Christ himself. If you need indulgences, absolution, remission, satisfaction, or purgation, you can find it laid up in Christ: "Our whole salvation and all its parts are comprehended in Christ."

Michael Horton has noted that Calvin's "real genius is to be found in his remarkable ability to synthesize the best thought of the whole Christian tradition and sift it with rigorous exegetical skill and evangelical instincts."[3] We see that synthetic genius at work here. In this brief survey of union with Christ we have Calvin's whole strategy of reformation in a microcosm: leveraging the central, most catholic elements of the church's creedal heritage to critique and displace contemporary deviations. His goal was to teach union with Christ in a way that equipped believers to find all they need in Christ as the great church has classically confessed him.

The Structure of Union with Christ

In his next move, Calvin makes explicit what we might call the "structure" of union with Christ. Recall that the Apostles' Creed itself leaves the move from the second article to the third article somewhat

3. Horton, *Calvin on the Christian Life*, 17.

implicit. Calvin draws it out dramatically, using his expertise in the rhetorical methods of Renaissance humanism. Having described how salvation is all in Christ, he now sets Christ off as if at a distance from us, for us to consider. This strategic pedagogical move, of positing a conceptual interval between the salvation worked out in Christ on one side, and our inclusion in it on the other, draws our attention to the decisive issue of how that gap is filled. Here is how Calvin puts it:

> First, we must understand that as long as Christ remains outside of us, and we are separated from him, all that he has suffered and done for the salvation of the human race remains useless and of no value for us. Therefore, to share with us what he has received from the Father, he had to become ours and to dwell within us.[4]

This "become ours" is Calvin's shorthand for everything about the great exchange accomplished by union with Christ, and he briefly lists other elements of salvation like Christ becoming our head and the firstborn among many children and our being engrafted into him, putting on Christ, and growing into one body with him.[5]

How does this all-important inclusion in Christ come about? The Protestant answer is "by faith," and Calvin immediately provides that answer. But he provides it in a way that also moves the reader on to a higher answer, one on which faith itself depends:

> It is true that we obtain this by faith. Yet since we see that not all indiscriminately embrace that communion with Christ which is offered through the gospel, reason itself teaches us to climb higher and to examine into the secret energy of the Spirit by which we come to enjoy Christ and all his benefits. . . . To sum up, the Holy Spirit is the bond by which Christ effectually unites us to himself.[6]

4. Calvin, *Institutes of the Christian Religion* III.1.1, 537.
5. Calvin, *Institutes of the Christian Religion* III.1.1, 537. The McNeill/Battles edition gives the Scripture references for these individual phrases as Eph. 4:15; Rom. 8:29; Rom. 11:17; Gal. 3:27, though Calvin is casting a wider linguistic net than just these passages.
6. Calvin, *Institutes of the Christian Religion* III.1.1, 537–38.

There are two things to notice here about the structure of union with Christ, one in the vertical dimension and one in the horizontal. Vertically, Calvin directs our attention upward, from the act of faith by which we obtain union with Christ to the heavenly reality of the Third Person of the Trinity, the Holy Spirit. The Spirit provides the "secret energy" of our faith in Christ. This movement of thought is a trinitarian tour de force. It directs our attention to the work of the Trinity in saving faith: the Father has given all blessings to the incarnate Son, in whom we believe by the power of the Spirit. It is a vision of salvation that is simultaneously Christ-centered and Trinity-centered, because it traces the work of the Father and the Spirit in constituting the Son as our salvation and bringing us into union with him.

But Calvin's description also sets up a horizontal dynamic, according to which a certain distance stretches out between us and Christ: the Father deposits salvation in Christ during his life as narrated in the Gospels, but "as long as Christ remains outside of us, and we are separated from him," everything he did in that life "remains useless and of no value for us." Chronologically, most believers come along later on the timeline and are separated from the life of Jesus by a span of years. But the real gap or separation is one that applied even to the contemporaries of the incarnate Son "in the days of his flesh."[7] Those contemporaries (including of course the original disciples) needed the life of Christ to take place not just alongside them but within them. So the soteriological gap that Calvin sketches out is a conceptual one, between our salvation as it exists in Christ himself (deposited there by the Father, stored up in the Son) and our lives considered as being discontinuous, distant, or external to his (see the figure on p. 60). Calvin poses the question, What closes this gap? The answer to the horizontal dimension is the same as it was for the vertical dimension: faith, brought about by the Holy Spirit.

---

7. The phrase "in the days of his flesh" can be misinterpreted in several ways, but it is worth retaining simply because it is the way Heb. 5:7 characterizes the life of Jesus before his resurrection and ascension.

The structure of union with Christ is therefore trinitarian, and the Holy Spirit plays the crucial role in bringing about our inclusion in the blessings that the Father has stored up in the Son. Considered in its horizontal dimension, the structure of union with Christ forces us to consider with complete seriousness how the gap between us and Christ is closed. If the life of Christ remains external to us, we do not take part in the salvation it contains.

Sketching out the structure of union is instructionally helpful, but the distance itself is more than pedagogical. In terms of the spiritual life of Christians, hardly anything matters more than a consistent grasp of the fact that this gap is closed by faith, worked by the Spirit. This answer is full, comprehensive, and exclusive: no other answer can be added, lest it subtract from the one true pneumatological answer. Pastorally speaking, souls are burdened and lives are compromised to the extent that Christians permit themselves to set any other reality into this gap in order to fill it up. Good works, moral worthiness, passionate personal experiences, mystical insights, theological education, loyal membership, and many other things, however good in themselves and necessary in their proper places, are detrimental and counterproductive if pressed into service here. Nothing else unites believers to the salvation that the Father has placed in the Son except the Holy Spirit.

Although this structure of union is universally Christian—it is recognizably the one Christian soteriology of union with Christ, in diagrammatic form—there is nevertheless some variety in the way it is characterized and conceived. Calvin himself states it with an identifiably Protestant accent: his opening gambit is "faith alone," which opens out onto a confession of the work of the Spirit alone.

Furthermore, Calvin builds out the rest of his *Institutes* according to this distinction. The hinge we have just examined turns the corner to book III, *The Way in Which We Receive the Grace of Christ: What Benefits Come to Us from It, and What Effects Follow*. Here he discusses soteriology proper, including regeneration, mortification, vivification, justification, prayer, and election. It is not until the final book, book IV, that he takes up the topics of *The External Means or Aids by Which God Invites Us into the Society of Christ and Holds Us Therein*. Here, not under the heading of actual ways "in which we receive the grace," but under the heading of "external means or aids," Calvin takes up the topics of the church, its legitimate teaching authority, the sacraments, and civil government. Does this organizational schema demote church and sacrament too far? Certainly his ecclesiology and sacramentology are quite robust, and no reasonable reader could take Calvin to be defending a kind of Christian existence for which church and sacrament are merely optional. Nevertheless, it is hard to imagine a Roman Catholic catechist putting off discussion of the church and sacrament for so long, or failing to emphasize their structural role in the actual "way in which we receive the grace of Christ" in the first place. It is easy to imagine similar adjustments or accents that might be introduced by other traditions. The Eastern Orthodox, Baptists, Lutherans, and Anglicans could gather around a diagram of the structure of union with Christ and have a lively set of agreements and disagreements regarding where to locate, how to describe, and how much to emphasize the key soteriological topics we expect them to cherish.

Some disagreements matter more than others, of course—and one of the main things Christians disagree with one another about is how much they disagree. Our diagram of the structure of union with Christ (see p. 60), taken in its most abstractly formal sense and with nothing labeled, could in fact be subject to radically diverse interpretations. If someone who believes that Jesus Christ was nothing more than a great role model were to interpret it, they would consider his life on the left side to be a great example, the life on the right side to be one that should follow his pattern, and the gap between them would be nothing more than the question of what motivations would empower perfect imitation. Such a nonsupernatural interpretation would rightly be judged radically sub-Christian. It would be such a misconstrual of the very nature and meaning of salvation that its suggestions for how to bridge the gap would be necessarily off the mark.

There are in fact extreme disagreements about the character of the Christian religion, and they can be compared by considering the content of union with Christ. An especially sharp contrast is drawn by Anglican E. A. Litton (1813–97) between the soteriological vision of the Church of England's Thirty-Nine Articles and the Roman Catholic theology of the nineteenth century. Litton wrote an introduction to theology with a special interest in drawing out this contrast systemically, from first principles. Here is how he contrasted the two systems: "Romanism (including its mutilated counterpart, Anglo-Catholicism) is a religion of the incarnation, the virtue of which is communicated by sacraments; Protestantism is a religion of the atonement, the virtue of which is appropriated by direct faith in Christ, His Word and His works."[8] It is easy to see how these two systems differ in their construals of union with Christ. If Christianity is "a religion of the incarnation," then the operative question becomes how to participate in that reality; sacramental mediation would accordingly be utterly central and would carry the real content of the religion. Litton's language makes it clear that he intends to draw out the difference as contrastively as possible (and to take sides, obviously), but he also freely admits that neither side simply denies what the other affirms. It is not as if Roman Catholic theology rejects the atonement or Protestant theology rejects the incarnation:

> On neither side are these cordial facts of religion, or their connection, denied; there could have been no atonement, if there had not been an incarnation; but the stress laid on the one or the other, and

8. Litton, *Introduction to Dogmatic Theology*, xxi.

particularly differences of view as regards the instrument of appropriation, may affect our whole conception of Christianity and lead to widely divergent theological systems.[9]

In Litton's intentionally polemical way of putting it, we note that disagreement about what fills the gap is actually disagreement about what the gap even is. In the classical Protestant view, which we will develop further in chapter 4, the incarnation is foundational for the atonement. When the Son takes human nature into union with himself personally, he establishes a certain union with us. So it can never be a matter of choosing between the incarnation and the atonement. But even on what Litton identifies as the Roman Catholic view, the incarnation as it actually took place is confessed as being ordered to the atonement. The problem of sin was at the very least a blockage that had to be removed before fallen humanity could participate in Christ's renewal of human nature.

It is important to strike the right balance here between unity and variety and to establish an adequate scale for assessing these differences. If the one central reality of soteriology is union with Christ, and its underlying structure raises the question of how we come to participate in that salvation (that is, what bridges the gap), then our ways of filling out the picture matter a great deal. There is ample room to air sharp disagreements and no need to deny or conceal differences. But centered on union with Christ, we will be in a better position to be precise about what is at stake.

The Scope and Weight of Union with Christ

We have argued that the Christian doctrine of salvation needs to remain resolutely centered on union with Christ. But now we must take another step and characterize not just the centrality but the massiveness of that commitment to union with Christ. We must specify

9. Litton, *Introduction to Dogmatic Theology*, xxi–xxii.

that there is also a necessarily vast scope and scale of commitment to union with Christ. Even if the doctrine of union with Christ is securely in place, it cannot do its necessary work in the Christian theological system if it is treated as something spiritually small. In fact, unless the doctrine is sufficiently large and weighty, it will not remain central. The doctrine of union with Christ must have gravity to remain the orbital center of the system.

This is worth insisting on because there is a recurring temptation in Christian thought to continue using the language of union with Christ while diminishing its meaning. The "in Christ" terminology, abundantly present in Scripture and unavoidably widespread in tradition, may be picked up and used, but in a setting and with presuppositions that allow it to mean only something rather weightless. It is possible to speak of salvation in terms of union with Christ while the real center of soteriological gravity lies elsewhere. It is possible to work out the real business of salvation in some other set of terms and presuppositions and only then to introduce the category of union with Christ as a kind of ornamental flourish. When this happens, a kind of respectful honor is paid to the verbiage of union, an honor that gives the illusion of all things being well. But unless the doctrine of union with Christ is doing the actual work in an account of salvation, this ornamental use of "in Christ" terminology is a subterfuge. All the terminology of union with Christ may be left in place but redefined in a diminished way. "Diminishment" is the key term. Soteriological schemes whose centers of gravity lie elsewhere almost inevitably fall prey to a kind of entropic force or orbital decay. They usually terminate in a construal of the Christian life that dissipates into the merely natural. Moralism, legalism, and formalism take over.

William Sherlock

We could illustrate this tendency with various forms of theological liberalism. Any attempt to describe the Christian life in nonsupernatural terms is bound to relegate union with Christ to little more than a figure of speech. But the temptation is not limited to the ranks of starkly antisupernaturalist modernist theologians. In fact, the most striking historical example of a theological schema that functionally diminished union with Christ while still using all the right words is the seventeenth-century moralizing rationalism championed by William Sherlock (1639–1707). Sherlock was a priest in the Church of England at a time that many would consider the golden age of Puritan spiritual and devotional writing. John Owen and Thomas Goodwin were among the writers producing practical divinity of lasting value during this era. Sherlock, for his part, considered this variety of evangelical piety to be overheated and overwrought.[10] What he especially disagreed with was the way these intense devotional writers depicted union with Christ.

Though Sherlock set himself against a number of writers, it was John Owen's *Communion with God* that especially provoked him to write his deflationary account of union with Christ.[11] In the long middle section of *Communion with God*, Owen argues that salvation consists in personal union with the Son of God and that a great part of true religion consists in cultivating communion with him. The union itself is mystical—that is, secret and mysterious precisely because it is God's work. In awe of that mystical union, the Christian carries out particular exercises of communion or devotion to Christ. Owen's argument is deeply traditional, taking the form of devotional commentary on the language of the Song of Songs. In many ways, this christological section of his book reads like an extended Reformed

10. The story of Sherlock versus the Puritans on mystical union is told briefly in Lim, *Mystery Unveiled*, 204–14. Even more helpful is Fesko, "Communion Controversy." Fesko reports on a remarkable flurry of a dozen publications on this controversy in the 1670s by numerous authors, including works with polemical titles like *Sherlocismus Enervatus*. Sherlock's rationalistic theological agenda also involved him in a complicated dispute about the doctrine of the Trinity. See also Dixon, *Nice and Hot Disputes*, 109–37.

11. Sherlock, *Knowledge of Jesus Christ*. Owen's *Of Communion with God the Father, Son, and Holy Ghost* was published in 1657. It can be found in *The Works of John Owen*, ed. William H. Goold (London: Johnstone & Hunter, 1850), vol. 2. This edition, reprinted by the Banner of Truth Trust, includes nearly one hundred pages of "A Vindication of Some Passages . . . from the Exceptions of William Sherlock."

gloss on Bernard of Clairvaux's classic sermons on the Song of Songs. On page after page, Owen simply applies the Puritan distinction between union and communion to the medieval Christ-devotion.

But Sherlock objected, saying that this way of talking makes the Christian religion depend altogether on "the person of Christ" rather than on his gospel. Focusing on the person of Christ is, according to Sherlock, fanciful and dangerous. The underlying problem is the "mystical" in mystical union: Sherlock did not favor treating union with Christ as mystical at all. According to him, the Christian religion consists in believing the gospel message of Jesus Christ, becoming his disciple, and being a member of the church he established. "Let us all fetch our Religion from the plain Doctrines and Precepts of the Gospel of Christ, not from any pretended Personal Acquaintance with him."[12] Christ put himself fully into his gospel, and anybody who claims to stand in some kind of relation to the person of Christ is simply adding flowery language to the plain truth.

Sherlock was well aware that Scripture speaks of union with Christ, being in Christ, and abiding in Christ. But in each case he interpreted the language as referring not to any mystical encounter with Christ as a person but to a nonmysterious belief in Christ's teachings, obedience to his authority, and joining his church. To his credit, his emphasis on the church puts Sherlock in a position to prioritize the church over the individual, and as a result he gets hold of several passages of Scripture by the right end. But he is not content with merely showing this larger context. Instead, he develops the point polemically, always using his arguments to exclude any actual encounter with the person of Christ. This is evident in Sherlock's interpretation of Jesus's words in John 15:5, "I am the vine; you are the branches. Whoever abides in me and I in him, he it is that bears much fruit, for apart from me you can do nothing." To abide in Christ must mean, according to Sherlock, to abide in

12. Sherlock, *Knowledge of Jesus Christ*, 97.

his church: "It is evident from this very Chapter, that when Christ speaks in the first Person, *I* and *In me*, he cannot mean this of his *own Person*, but of his *Church, Doctrine, and Religion*."[13] Sherlock is insistent that Christ must be speaking of his church rather than of his person, because he sees no way of making sense of a personal union. Adopting a tone of incredulity, Sherlock presses his critique: "I would willingly learn what sense can be made of this, if we understand it of the *Person of Christ*: for it is not very intelligible, how we can *be* or *abide in* the *Person of Christ*; and it is more unintelligible still, how *we* can be in the *Person of Christ*, and the *Person of Christ* at the *same time be in us*, which is a new Piece of Philosophy, called Penetration of dimensions."[14] Since none of this is logically possible or even "very intelligible," Sherlock systematically replaces these ideas with church, profession of faith, belief in doctrine, and obedience to precept. It is a remarkable conceptual paraphrase, and Sherlock carries it out consistently:

> But if by *He that abideth in me*, we understand the *Christian Church*, i.e. he who makes a publick and visible profession of Faith *in me*, and continues in Society with those, who do so; and by *I in him*, the *Christian Doctrine*, both the Sense and Reason of it is very evident: the sense is this; That Church which owns my Doctrine and Religion, is the *true Vine*, and all you who make a Publick Profession of Faith *in me* (of a belief of my Gospel) and live in Communion with one another, are the *Branches* in this Vine; and whoever of you continue stedfast in this Profession and Communion, and do not only make a visible profession of Faith in me, but suffer my Doctrine and Precepts to dwell and abide in you, to govern your Will and Affections, and to direct your Conversation in the World, all such of you will be very fruitful in good Works. . . . So that to *abide in Christ*, is to make a publick and visible Profession of Faith in Christ, to be the Members of his visible Church.[15]

13. Sherlock, *Knowledge of Jesus Christ*, 147 (italics original).
14. Sherlock, *Knowledge of Jesus Christ*, 147 (italics original).
15. Sherlock, *Knowledge of Jesus Christ*, 147–48 (italics original).

Sherlock carried out a relentless deflation of all the biblical metaphors and symbols for union with Christ. There is no biblical expression that he could not paraphrase into a merely moralistic and rationalistic interpretation; everything came to mean assent, obedience, and church membership.

Sherlock considered this deflation to be a necessary task precisely because, on his view, the Puritan devotional writers were guilty of overinflating the sense of the biblical language. Their characteristic pitch of interpretation consisted "in wresting metaphorical, and allusive expressions" from an obvious and public sense to a individual and mystical sense. "When the Scripture describes the profession of Christianity, a sincere belief and obedience to the Gospel, by having Christ, and being *in* Christ, and coming to him, and receiving him, these men expound these phrases . . . to signifie, I know not what unintelligible Union, and spiritual progress and closure of the Soul with him; An Union of Persons, instead of an agreement in faith and manners."[16]

Perhaps the lowest moment in Sherlock's rhetorical revolution is when he extrapolates from his favorite word, "public" (or "publick"), to the more comprehensive word "political": "The nature of this Union between Christ and the Christian Church, which is not a natural, but a *Political* Union."[17] In contrast to a mystical reality to be experienced spiritually in personal faith, Sherlock defines union with Christ at the far extreme of political union, "that is such an Union, as is between *a Prince* and *his Subjects*." On this view, "Christ is *a spiritual King*, and all Christians are his *Subjects*, and our Union to Christ consists in our belief of his Revelations, obedience to his Laws, and subjection to his Authority."[18] For anyone with a higher view of union with Christ, the disappointment is palpable.

---

16. Sherlock, *Knowledge of Jesus Christ*, 108–9 (italics original).
17. Sherlock, *Knowledge of Jesus Christ*, 156 (italics original).
18. Sherlock, *Knowledge of Jesus Christ*, 156 (italics original).

Edward Polhill

Sherlock's reduction of union with Christ to mere political union called forth a volley of refutations.[19] Edward Polhill's (predictably titled) *Answer to the Discourse of Mr. William Sherlock* has the honor of being the most comprehensive in its outlook and the most thorough in its analysis. Polhill (1622–94) responds to Sherlock's book nearly paragraph by paragraph, and his refutation runs to 621 pages as compared to Sherlock's 432. The quote-and-response format becomes admittedly tedious, and Polhill writes in such earnest that he sometimes descends nearly into bluster. Reacting to Sherlock's assertion that basing religion on the person of Christ is "fanciful," Polhill responds, "Fanciful! Alas! That a Christian, a Divine, should let drop such a reproachful word, on so sacred a thing as the Application of Christ!"[20] But his main point is that the Sherlockian deflation of union with Christ made tatters of the biblical witness. Scripture itself had to "labour under very odd Glosses" to be brought down to the level of political union, mere assent, and simple obedience.[21] So in hand-to-hand—or verse-to-verse—combat Polhill undertakes to restore the depth and fullness of union to the whole catalog of biblical terms: Christ as the head of the body, the vine of the branches, the one who dwells in believers and in whom believers dwell, the one who knows and is known by his disciples in all ages, and so on. This real, spiritual union with the person of Christ has to be kept in place as the foundation of all the things Sherlock himself wanted, for on it is built all the other goods: assent to Christ's teaching, trust in his gospel,

---

19. See Fesko, "Communion Controversy," for a good discussion of John Owen's response to Sherlock and a full bibliography of Sherlock's opponents. As Fesko points out, the whole controversy deserves more attention. Here I am focusing only on the nature of union with Christ, but Sherlock's motivations included a settled opposition to dissenters (on political grounds) and to Reformed soteriology (on theological grounds). He was the kind of moralist who distrusted an emphasis on justification by grace, especially if it included the idea of imputed righteousness. As a result, both he and his (dissenting Calvinist) opponents tended to thrash around rather widely in argument.

20. Polhill, *Answer to Sherlock*, 18.

21. Polhill, *Answer to Sherlock*, 18.

obedience to his commands, and membership in his church. These goods have to follow from and presuppose the union. Even "political union" is something a believer can enjoy, but only on the basis of real, spiritual union. "A belief of Revelations is only a dogmatical faith, which is found in many not united to Christ; Obedience is not our mystical union to Christ, but a fruit of it; Christ and the Soul being once espoused, out-comes a blessed progeny of good works."[22]

There is some abiding value to the controversy Sherlock stirred up. He was so drastically and consistently wrong about union with Christ that his reductive, minimizing account of the doctrine is an abiding cautionary tale. This otherwise forgettable seventeenth-century theological conflict stands as a clear example of how high the stakes are for the doctrine. Sherlock attacked and was counterattacked; both sides produced the back-and-forth fusillade of polemical literature that only a historian of pamphlet wars could love. This goes for the anti-Sherlock volleys from very famous theologians like John Owen as well as for deep thinkers like Edward Polhill. But Polhill, at least, seems to have recognized that he buried some of his most important theological points in a sprawling 1675 tome with an easily ignorable title (*An Answer to the Discourse of Mr. William Sherlock* is not exactly catchy). Five years later, he took up the same subject but had the wisdom to write out his views constructively and systematically. Leaving behind the cut-and-thrust of polemics, never mentioning Sherlock by name, and reducing the bulk of his book by half, Polhill set forth his view of union with Christ in the minor masterpiece *Christus in Corde, or, The Mystical Union Between Christ and Believers.*[23]

Cleaned up from the dust of controversy, Polhill's approach to the doctrine is admirable. It is in every way a model of giving union with Christ the magnitude and influence it deserves in Christian thought.

22. Polhill, *Answer to Sherlock*, 194.

23. This important treatise was for some reason omitted from the single-volume *Works of Edward Polhill* published in 1678, republished by Thomas Ward and Co. in 1844, and kept in print by Soli Deo Gloria Publications since 1998. As a result, even the small number of readers who know Polhill at all do not usually know *Christus in Corde.*

Polhill presents the believer's mystical union with Christ as utterly mysterious, in fact as one of the three great mysteries of the Christian system. The highest mystery of unity is the Trinity itself, the central mystery of salvation is the joining of divinity and humanity in the incarnation, and the nearest mystery to us is the union of Christ and believers.[24] Union with Christ keeps company with Trinity and incarnation. Polhill carefully notes the differences among these three unions and avoids the error of exalting human salvation to some level of equal ultimacy with the divine. But by associating soteriology with Trinity and incarnation, he imparts an aura of true theological mystery into soteriology. The Son of God stands at the center of all three mysteries, as the center of the Trinity, the person of the hypostatic union, and the savior to whom the believer is united. From this exalted point of view, Polhill takes up the task of explaining the ways God speaks about union with Christ in the Scriptures. "Because this mystery is very deep," he says, God reveals it strategically:

> The Holy Ghost, in condescension to our weakness, shadows out this Union by many earthly patterns, *viz.* by the Law-union of a King and Subjects; by the Love-union of an Husband and Wife; by the Artificial union of the Foundation and Building; by the Natural union of the Vine and Branches, the Head and Members; by the intimate union and incorporation of the Food and the Body. There is that in the Mystical union which answer; to all these earthly patterns; and withal, that which as much exceeds them, as a substance doth a shadow.[25]

Union with Christ is a reality so high and exalted that it cannot be represented directly. Instead, God hints at it, symbolizes it, and shadows it forth using a range of images. None of these images capture the

---

24. Polhill, *Christus in Corde*, unnumbered page of preface.
25. Polhill, *Christus in Corde*, unnumbered page of preface. Though Polhill has left Sherlock behind him, alert readers will see that he incorporates Sherlock's "Law-union," or political union, into his more comprehensive account.

full reality of the mystical union, but God has given each of them to us as partial indications of the profound reality itself.

In each of these revealed images, the analogical structure is of something similar and something that goes beyond the similarity. Polhill deftly picks out the leading point of analogy in each: "In the Political union we have Law and Power; in the Conjugal one, love; in the Architectonical one, support; in that of the Vine and Head, vital influence; in that of food, nourishment and intimate conjunction." But he always returns to the main point, that the union of Christ with the believer superabundantly contains all these benefits: "In the mystical union we have all these."[26] And yet the mystical union has to do with Christ, and in "every way he hath the preeminence over the earthly patterns."[27] Therefore "that union . . . which fully answers to so many resemblances of different import, must needs be a very mysterious one."[28]

Polhill's presentation of union with Christ is exemplary on all fronts. We have seen how he secures its greatness and centrality in the Christian account of salvation. We have seen how he develops this further by deploying a sophisticated interpretation of the breadth of the Bible's metaphorical witness. But before taking our leave of his *Christus in Corde*, we should note that his radical Christocentrism is not at odds with a fully trinitarian focus. We have already seen how he associates the mystery of soteriological union with the higher mysteries of incarnation and Trinity. But it is also worth noting how careful he is, in his exploration of the biblical metaphors, to guide his readers to see the Holy Spirit at work in this union. Indeed, the Spirit is in some ways the real substance and life of union with Christ. Polhill brings this out with special clarity in considering the vine-to-branch relation of union: "There is a supply of the Holy Spirit from Christ unto Believers; he is made sanctification to them; he lives in them; there is an effectual working in every one of them; and all this is by

26. Polhill, *Christus in Corde*, 140.
27. Polhill, *Christus in Corde*, 141.
28. Polhill, *Christus in Corde*, 140.

the Spirit communicated from him the Root and Head of all Grace."[29] Furthermore, Polhill makes it clear that not just some effects of the Spirit are communicated but that "the Spirit itself is communicated to Believers."[30] He shows some awareness of how large a claim this is, and he grounds it in a full trinitarian account of salvation: if we ask "in what sense the Spirit it self is communicated to them," we must "first take notice of three memorable expressions in Scripture; That is, the *sending of the Spirit*, the *giving of the Spirit*, the *dwelling* or *inhabiting of the Spirit in us*."[31] The sending is obviously a piece of trinitarian theology stretching back through the mission of the Holy Spirit to his eternal origin from the Father and the Son; the giving is the experienced, salvation-historical result of that properly trinitarian mission; and the inhabiting is the supernatural point of contact with the believer.

Theological Genres and Schemas for Union with Christ

Having considered the structure of union with Christ, as well as its scope and weight within a theological system, we can also consider the question of the genres in which the doctrine can be expressed effectively. In chapter 2 we traced the two most fundamental genres: Gospel and epistle. These are, so to speak, God's own genres for communicating union with Christ. On that canonical foundation, we now consider what genres constitute the most appropriate format for contemporary accounts of union with Christ.

There are historical examples of theological writing that follow, in a variety of ways, the biblical contours already traced: giving attention first to the life of Jesus and then to its application to us, or our inclusion within it. We will move quickly through some examples of theological writing from the history of the church, with the goal not just of surveying what has been done in the past but of considering

29. Polhill, *Christus in Corde*, 156.
30. Polhill, *Christus in Corde*, 162.
31. Polhill, *Christus in Corde*, 179–80 (italics original).

possibilities for future theological writing on the doctrine of salvation. Guiding questions for us will be: What literary form will enable us to write evangelical soteriology of a kind that fixes our attention on Jesus Christ primarily while effectively delivering the results needed for explicit soteriological teaching and also describing the experience of salvation? And how should we combine narrative and argumentative exposition in soteriology?

First and most importantly, there is the tradition of writing meditatively on the sequence of individual events of the life of Jesus. In its high medieval development, this tradition is known as the "mysteries of the life of Christ." It has a rich heritage in devotional writing about Jesus. It may be best enshrined in poetic forms like the medieval passion plays or in devotional forms like the sequence of mysteries remembered in the rosary and its prayers. On a very large scale, a significant portion of the church's liturgical year is patterned on major events in the life of Christ. As a result, the structure of the life of Jesus is imprinted on numerous liturgical forms and filters into lectionaries, sermon sequences, and other forms of church life. At their best, all these representational genres display the two moments of the soteriology of union with Christ: first the life of Christ, then our inclusion within it. But without denigrating devotional writing, artistic expressions, or liturgical forms, we do need to press forward to a kind of theological writing that not only bears the imprints of the life of Christ and our inclusion in it but also takes up the work of analyzing it conceptually.

Thomas Aquinas and the Mysteries of the Life of Christ

In terms of theological writing, this "mysteries of the life of Christ" tradition reaches a kind of classic statement in the third part of Thomas Aquinas's *Summa Theologiae*.[32] Within the *Summa Theolo-*

---

32. Very much worth mentioning is a Franciscan text known as the *Meditations on the Life of Christ*, long attributed to Bonaventure but probably not actually his work. It follows a livelier narrative and is written more simply, so it does not rise to the same heights

giae part III, all of questions 27 to 45 are taken up with individual events from Jesus's life, examined from a variety of angles for their theological, spiritual, and moral pertinence. This series of questions stands out in the *Summa* for being marked by close exegesis—that is, by following the text of Scripture more directly. Thomas takes up an event and asks why it happened the way it did, what it signifies, and how it is related to the triune God's overall saving work through the instrument of Christ's human life. There is a richness of detail in these sections that is driven by an underlying Augustinian conviction: in a sermon on John 6, Augustine remarks that "since Christ is Himself the Word of God, even the deeds of the Word are a word for us."[33] That is, each action of Christ is eloquent in itself; his actions carry meaning and can be exegeted as communication of truth. On the basis of this conviction, Thomas approaches these mysteries as the place where the very content of our knowledge of Christ is to be contemplated. The events themselves are eloquent, and Christ is present to us in them. This explains why, in a comment on Ephesians 3, Aquinas points to this sequence of events to answer the question of how we can know the love of Christ, which surpasses knowledge. His answer reaches out to a consideration of the events of the Gospels: "To know Christ's love is to know all the mysteries of Christ's Incarnation and our Redemption. These have poured out from the immense charity of God; a charity exceeding every created intelligence and the [combined] knowledge of all of them because it cannot be grasped in thought."[34] Thomas comes to these mysteries, then, with high expectation that each of them is a word of infinite depth, and he brings to bear on their interpretation all of his theological acumen.

---

as Thomas's treatment in the *Summa Theologiae*. Even before the advent of printing, the *Meditations* circulated as an illustrated text and exerted a great influence on the visual arts as the Renaissance approached. A good version of the illustrated *Meditations* is Green and Ragusa, *Meditations on the Life of Christ*.

33. Augustine, *Homilies on the Gospel of John, 1–40*, Homily 24 (424). In context, Augustine is speaking about Christ's miracles, but the principle applies to all his works.

34. Thomas Aquinas, *Commentary on Saint Paul's Epistle to the Ephesians*, 144.

That theological acumen, throughout the entire treatise on the events of Christ's incarnate ministry, is guided by the notion of fittingness. That is, rather than arguing about what necessarily must be the case, Thomas asks of each event why it is fitting, or appropriate, that this thing should have been done this way. The logic of fittingness is extremely flexible because it is designed not so much to produce proofs or to establish doctrines as to give further insight into the why and the how of what has happened. Given that God could have done things in various ways, what is particularly made known in God's free choice to do this thing in this way? Thomas pursues these questions in ways that can seem childish: Why did Jesus live to early middle age rather than complete his work earlier? Why didn't he live to an older age? The questions sometimes seem, if not playful, at least less than urgent. But because Thomas is seeking the wisdom of appropriateness, the questions always yield deeper insight into the unique character of the one mystery of the incarnate life through the prism of one particular event. The "mysteries of the life of Christ" tradition is a great one, which Roman Catholic theology has tried to revive in the twentieth century with a variety of results.[35]

Petrus van Mastricht on the Life of the Mediator

There is a Protestant version of this tradition that can be traced in the works of a number of post-Reformation dogmaticians from the period of Protestant Scholasticism. Petrus van Mastricht, in his sprawling and detailed Reformed Christology, devotes ample space to theological consideration of these mysteries under the heading of "The Life of the Mediator."[36] His key presuppositions about the

35. The European discussion was important but had limited impact in English-language theology. See Grillmeier, "Mit ihm und in ihm." Several works available in English that partially follow the "mysteries of the life" format are Guardini, *The Lord*; Joseph Ratzinger's three-volume *Jesus of Nazareth*; Thomas Weinandy's three-volume *Jesus Becoming Jesus*; and Legge, *Trinitarian Christology of St. Thomas Aquinas*.

36. Mastricht, *Theoretical-Practical Theology*, 4:291–582. Within Mastricht's elaborate organizational schema, he uses the term "life of the mediator" as a term of art to indicate

events of the life of Jesus surface in his decision to set the discussion under the rubric of 2 Corinthians 4:10: "That the life of Jesus might be made manifest in our body."[37] Mastricht considers the various possible meanings of the phrase "the life of Jesus," one of which is the biographical series of events narrated in the Gospels. Mastricht is fully aware that what he is about to undertake is a detailed consideration of that series of events. But here at the outset he considers how, in Paul's phrasing, "the life of Jesus" signifies "his internal life, whether the potency or the efficacy of living, whereby he also lives in us (Gal. 2:20), whereby from our mystical union with him, he confers to us the strength to work spiritually, for which reason he is called our life (Col. 3:4)."[38] Mastricht's approach is from the outset a spiritual, or applied, approach to the task of contemplating the events of Jesus's life. As a result, he is able to work out a robust and well-rounded soteriology—salvation both accomplished and applied—in the genre of tracing Jesus's steps from beginning to end. At its best, as in Mastricht, the Protestant version of the "mysteries of the life of Christ" tradition is a powerfully consolidated extrapolation of the Gospels-then-epistles structure of salvation. It is an organizational schema that imparts to systematic soteriology a definite narrative shape while leaving ample room for application. It keeps Jesus central in soteriology even at the genre level; it keeps the "Christ" in "union with Christ."

It is no accident that the two best resources we have highlighted, Thomas's *Summa Theologiae* and Mastricht's *Theoretical-Practical Theology*, are both rather large multivolume theological works. The theology of the mysteries of the life of Christ is carried out almost exclusively in large books. Following the approach of the mysteries requires a lot of pages, partly because there are many events to ponder and partly because each event is also unpacked and analyzed for its application to the believer. Recall that the "mysteries of the

---

only what happens between "the incarnation" (that is, conception and birth) and the death/resurrection (all the way to the seating at the right hand of the Father).

37. Mastricht, *Theoretical-Practical Theology*, 4:343–45.

38. Mastricht, *Theoretical-Practical Theology*, 4:344.

life of Christ" tradition is not so much a convention for organizing Christology for its own sake as much as it is a genre for leading the reader into understanding union with Christ. The fact that it focuses so directly on Jesus himself as it develops its theme of union with Christ is one of its great merits. As a genre for teaching union with Christ, the "mysteries of the life of Christ" tradition has some obvious similarities with the canonical Gospels.

Isaac Ambrose on Looking unto Jesus

Having begun by considering works so seriously and elaborately theological, we may come back down the scale of difficulty just a few steps to a kind of writing that, while far more devotional than Aquinas and Mastricht, is nevertheless carefully focused on theology. We could have started at the lower end of the devotional scale, with very simple spiritual writing, and worked our way up gradually. But descending from the Scholastic heights is a more instructive approach to the kind of theologically rich devotional writing we want to consider next as a genre for teaching union with Christ. The clearest and most extended example of this genre is the book *Looking unto Jesus* by Isaac Ambrose (1604–64). To call it devotional literature is to raise the category of devotional literature quite high indeed; *Looking unto Jesus* attains a standard to which most devotional writing can only aspire. Ambrose wrote it with the design of placing the minds of his readers in the presence of Jesus Christ. It is more than seven hundred pages long and demands close attention. But it trains the mind in how to consider Jesus in a way very few other books even attempt.

"Consider Jesus": one of the central distinctions Ambrose makes is between simply *knowing* something, on the one hand, and *considering* it, on the other. Both are modes of "looking unto Jesus," but considering a truth about Jesus is a step further than simply knowing it. Ambrose explains this distinction several times throughout the work, but he gives an especially clear restatement of it in the section on Christ's resurrection:

Variations on a Soteriological Theme 79

> It is not enough to know a saving necessary truth, but it is required farther that we digest truths and that we draw forth their strength for the nourishment and refreshing of our poor souls. As a man may in half an hour chew and take into his stomach that meat which he must have seven or eight hours at least to digest, so a man may take into his understanding more truths in an hour than he is able to digest well in many.
>
> What good those men are like to get by sermons or providences who are unaccustomed to this work of meditation, I cannot imagine. It is observed by some that this is the reason why so much preaching is lost amongst us; why professors that run from sermon to sermon and are never weary of hearing or reading have notwithstanding such languishing starved souls; because they will not meditate. And therefore God commanded Joshua not only to read the law but to consider of it and dwell upon it; "This book of the law shall not depart out of thy mouth but thou shalt meditate therein day and night" (Joshua 1:8). Why, this is the duty that I am now pressing to, if thou knowest these things, consider, ruminate, meditate, ponder on them again and again. And because this work requires enlargedness of heart and spirit, therefore take it into parts and consider of each of them apart by itself.[39]

This is a commendation of the spiritual discipline of meditation, and much of it would be at home in any book on spiritual disciplines. But Ambrose focuses on meditation on the consideration of events in the life of Christ, and the project of *Looking unto Jesus* is to guide the reader into contemplation of those events as the actual central act of the spiritual life. To look unto Jesus is a contemplative action that corresponds to the spiritual structure of salvation itself; it cognitively reenacts the movement of being taken into Christ.

Ambrose devotes about eighty pages of *Looking unto Jesus* to the resurrection; he directs readers to "consider, ruminate, meditate," and ponder this event. He has a great deal to say about how Christ carried

---

39. Ambrose, *Looking unto Jesus*, 466.

out salvation in his rising from the dead. But the point of devotional meditation on the moments of the life of Jesus is precisely to identify a great deal of subject matter; it is a genre for lovers.[40]

The backbone of Ambrose's book is the Gospels, taken more or less in a harmony as he tracks the events of the life of Jesus. The exercise is more or less synoptic. But his exposition draws on the depths of Old Testament theology, on the one hand, and the penetrating insight of the New Testament epistles, on the other hand, so its expansiveness permits it to be a study of the Gospels with sidelights and skylights open in all directions. It is also informed by classic Christian doctrine to a remarkable degree, not just in a broadly orthodox kind of way but in considerable detail. This is one of the features that makes Isaac Ambrose's model so attractive and promising as a possible genre for theological writing: it really gets theological.

Here are two examples, on two successive pages of the section on the resurrection. First, Christ's resurrection was not just his but ours as well. There are several ways Ambrose could have made this point, but when he reached into the conceptual toolkit to find the right way to do it, he came out with this:

Christ rose again as a common person, he stood in our stead, and therefore when he rose from death, we and all the church of Christ rose together with him and in him. We have formerly observed, that Christ took upon him the person of no man, he took only the nature of man into the union of the second person, that so he might die and rise again, not as a particular, but a common person, that he might be as a representative in our room and stead.[41]

What Ambrose is invoking here is not just the Christology of the Council of Chalcedon (451) but later elaborations of it from the next council (Constantinople II, 553) and from Leontius of Byzantium's

---

40. The next few paragraphs were first published in the form of a blog post at https://scriptoriumdaily.com/standard-toolkit/.

41. Ambrose, *Looking unto Jesus*, 418.

Variations on a Soteriological Theme

formula about the human nature of Jesus being enhypostatic: not personal in itself but only personal as the human nature of the Second Person of the Trinity. Ambrose rightly sees that the soteriological and devotional point he wants to make is supported by the conceptually elaborate post-Chalcedonian conciliar Christology.

Second, Christ rose by his own power. After proving this point from Scripture (John 2:19; 10:18), Ambrose admits, "Against this it may be objected, 'In many places, the resurrection of Christ is ascribed to his Father; how then is he said to raise up himself by his own power?'" Once again Ambrose reaches into the doctrinal toolkit and finds just what is needed for the job—the inseparable operations of the Trinity *ad extra*: "Christ's resurrection is the indivisible work of the blessed Trinity; it is a work common to all the three persons, there is but one power of the Father, and of the Son; so that of both is truly verified, the Father raised him, and the Son raised himself."[42] Again we see Ambrose making a spiritual and devotional point: the Son is Lord of his own resurrection. And again we see Ambrose supporting the point by taking immediate recourse to a pretty austere doctrine of God. And it works: the lordship of Christ simply must be grounded in the lordship of the one God, rather than worried over as if it contrasts or competes with the latter.

What is striking in both of these cases is that Ambrose does not seem to be working very hard at putting these doctrines in place. He calmly and serenely picks them up to explain his devotional point, presupposing that his Christian readers will be receptive to them, or even familiar with them ("we have formerly observed"). He takes up these doctrines with the deftness of long practice and applies them almost effortlessly to understanding how the resurrection of Jesus Christ can be an effective work for us and a manifestation of Christ's own lordship. Perhaps Ambrose's ability to take his readers so far into the details of Christology is related to his life-of-Jesus strategy. When the organizational principle of a theological project is so evident, a

---

42. Ambrose, *Looking unto Jesus*, 419.

82   Union with Christ and the Life of Faith

theologian or spiritual writer can venture further out into doctrinal
detail. When we consider how helpful the "mysteries of the life of
Christ" tradition is as a genre for presenting the soteriology of union
with Christ, we should also notice that it carries benefits for Christology proper, and for theological vigor in general. Founded securely on
the Gospels, a spiritual theology can extend further into systematic
clarification than might otherwise be tolerable for readers.

Thomas Goodwin on Setting Forth Christ in His Actions

There are some other Protestant treatises on salvation that follow
a plan somewhat similar to Ambrose's *Looking unto Jesus*. One excellent example is Thomas Goodwin's *Christ Set Forth*.[43] Goodwin's
project is not a meditation on the full range of Gospel events, but
only the final actions of death, resurrection, ascension, and enthronement. So it does not quite fit in the tradition of the "mysteries of the
life of Christ." But within his chosen range, Goodwin does follow
the pattern of taking up each event distinctly, drilling down into it
for soteriological gold, and moving through it at the leisurely pace
common to the mysteries genre. Goodwin is especially clear on the
purpose and the benefits of giving focused attention to each event in
turn. He is concerned with the spiritual danger of Christians focusing their attention on their own experiences of salvation. There are
believers, otherwise quite well grounded in the faith, "who yet in
the ordinary course and way of their spirits have been too much carried away with the rudiments of Christ in their own hearts, and not
after Christ himself."[44] His goal is to turn believers' attention toward
Christ directly, in the details of Christ working out their salvation in
himself. The point is not to seek Christ as some kind of purely objective reality at a distance from us, or to view him with disinterested

43. The treatise itself was originally published in 1642. The full scope of Goodwin's
scattered, multivolume project on soteriology has been traced helpfully by Carter, *Thomas
Goodwin on Union with Christ*.
44. Goodwin, *Christ Set Forth*, 3.

observation. The goal of the meditation remains soteriological: we want to see our salvation, but we want to see it first in him. Rather than believers "searching into the gracious dispositions of their own hearts," Goodwin wants them to take up "a more constant actual exercise of daily thoughts of faith towards Christ immediately."[45] Further, Goodwin can make room for the spiritual value of some introspection, because believers ought to examine their spiritual experience to discern whether the things they believe are truly making a difference in their own lives. But such introspection must remain in its proper place, which can only be secured by a prior focus on Christ himself. When Christians are overly focused on the ups and downs of their spiritual experience, they may think of themselves too highly or too lowly. "To rectify this error, the way is not wholly to reject all use of such evidences, but to order them," says Goodwin.[46] When theological works like Ambrose's *Looking unto Jesus* or Goodwin's *Christ Set Forth* establish good order among the spiritual priorities of the Christian life, this is not an accidental side effect. It is more nearly the whole point of the genre, and a central motive in its use through the ages. Devout attention follows the spiritual structure of salvation as union with Christ: first Christ working out our salvation, then our being included in him.

Jeremy Taylor's Theological Life of Christ

Jeremy Taylor's book *The Great Exemplar* is a three-volume work that has been hailed as one of the first lives of Christ in English. In some ways it clearly aligns with the "mysteries of the life of Christ" genre: it is soteriologically motivated rather than merely historical, it takes up distinct events in Jesus's life for meditative consideration, and it even provides "prayers fitted to the several mysteries" (in the words of the book's subtitle) for each of the events. It stands out from the mainstream tradition, though, because of how strictly focused it

45. Goodwin, *Christ Set Forth*, 3.
46. Goodwin, *Christ Set Forth*, 4.

is on imitating Christ. Taylor's title is to be taken seriously; it is more nearly a work on Christian ethics and morality than a work on soteriology proper. Its great benefit is its careful attention to the conduct of Christ as the foundation of our imitation of him as disciples. For this reason it serves as a helpful supplement to, or expansion of, the "mysteries of the life of Christ" tradition. It might be especially reassuring to readers who, sharing Sherlock's concern about antinomianism without falling into his opposite error of legalism, would like to see more of the ethical edge in the language of union and participation in Christ. But on its own, Taylor's *Exemplar* is overbalanced in the ethical direction, and most readers will find that imitation becomes so prominent that it obscures union.[47]

Joseph Hall's Contemplations

One of the finest pieces of writing in the mysteries tradition is in some ways an accidental entry into the genre. Anglican bishop Joseph Hall wrote a series of devout contemplations on narratives in Scripture, beginning with the creation.[48] About a third of his volume (roughly two hundred of six hundred pages) is devoted to the Gospels, tracking Christ from his conception to his ascension. Hall's contemplations on the life of Christ are wide-ranging and doctrinally savvy, drawing readers into the narrated moments of the life of Christ, where they discover that a place has been prepared for them.

Rudolf Stier on Every Word of Jesus

Another large-scale theological project that follows a different schema but still overlaps, as if by accident, with the "mysteries of the life of Christ" genre is Rudolf Stier's multivolume *Words of Jesus*

---

47. For a careful presentation of the proper relation of imitation and union, with particular interest in showing how they need not be mutually exclusive, see Hood, *Imitating God in Christ*.

48. Hall, *Contemplations on the Historical Passages of the Old and New Testaments*.

series.[49] Stier (1800–1862) set himself the task of commenting on every recorded word of Jesus, treating those words as God's direct self-revelation contained in books so divinely inspired that they repay close attention to every word. He took as his epigraph for the whole series Isaiah 52:6: "I am he that doth speak; behold it is I" (KJV). Stier organized his work as a kind of harmony of the Gospels but was closely attentive to how Jesus's words fit into the literary context of each Gospel. Mostly because of his commitment to taking every word into account, he would carefully compare pericopes and note subtle differences in Jesus's phraseology. Tracing the words of Jesus so closely obviously entails considering the various events of Jesus's life, though Stier's schema makes so much room for expounding Jesus's teachings that the biographical thread often vanishes for hundreds of pages at a time. Nevertheless, Stier's vivid sense that these words are not merely historical reportage, but exist in the ever-present now of the believing audience, leads him to treat Gospel words as the living speech of the risen Lord, present to his readers. In this way, Stier makes contact with the deep presupposition of the Gospel genre itself and aligns with the central impulse of the "mysteries of the life of Christ" tradition.

Further Variations on the Theme

Certain variations on the "mysteries of the life of Christ" genre are significant enough that we should probably consider them to be primarily instances of another impulse, or different ways of pursuing the soteriology of union with Christ. G. Campbell Morgan wrote a bestselling devotional book in the early twentieth century called *The Crises of the Christ*. His treatment follows the Gospels outline, paying special attention to those turning points that reveal new developments in salvation history. The material is richly sermonic and full of spiritual applications, but Morgan's main focus is not so much on

---

49. The series ran to eight volumes in German and was rapidly translated into English. The first volume is *The Words of Jesus*.

Christ as on the way God's plan moves forward decisively through his work. "The beauty of the life itself," he tells readers, "is only fully appreciated when it is seen as related in its every part to this mighty movement of God towards the redemption of man."[50] Readers familiar with the "mysteries of the life of Christ" genre will be able to see it peeking through over and over, but Morgan's soteriological center has more to do with a historical schema (covenantal or dispensational in a nontechnical sense) that spans the whole Bible. A more comprehensive approach to the project might be able to unite the two impulses, not only sketching out God's historical plan but also focusing it more directly on the way believers are included in the life of Christ.

Other variations worth noting, because they continue to be promising genres for theological instruction, include what we might call variations "from above"—works that intend to be primarily treatises on the divine attributes but that intentionally link themselves to the structure of the life of Christ as their way of displaying those attributes. A neglected classic of this type is Edward Polhill's *Speculum Theologiae in Christo: A View of Some Divine Truths Which Are Either Practically Exemplified in Jesus Christ Set Forth in the Gospel, or May Be Reasonably Deduced From Thence.*[51] Polhill treats Christ as a mirror in which we can see all the doctrines about God, or even as a book in which we can read the divine attributes written humanly: "In our Emmanuel we have a body of theology, an excellent summary of divine truths, in a very lively manner set forth to us. . . . Everything in Christ reads us a lecture of divinity."[52] The book is resolutely focused on soteriology, handling each divine attribute (wisdom, holiness, justice, love, power, truth, providence, grace, and so on) from the perspective

50. Morgan, *Crises of the Christ*, 15.

51. The work was originally published in 1678; the *Works of Edward Polhill* edition unfortunately fails to print the Latin title under which the English book was originally published, treating it as if its main title were *A View of Some Divine Truths* rather than *Speculum Theologiae in Christo*.

52. Polhill, *Speculum*, "To the Christian Reader," first unnumbered page.

of salvation. Furthermore, though treating Jesus Christ as a kind of living theology textbook might strike us as unpromising, Polhill carries out the project with wonderful attention to Christ's person and work. What he does not do, however, is follow out a chronological sequence of the mysteries of the life of Christ. Polhill consults the life of Jesus as a totality, indexing it to the divine attributes (which dictate his order of teaching). The result is still obviously a project about union with Christ, but coming down to it "from above" dictates a different genre decision. In this way, it reminds us of a vast body of other spiritual writing that also centers itself on union with Christ, but by following a different organizational schema. We might consider Christian devotional commentaries on the Song of Songs under this heading. They are organized as verse-by-verse expansions of the spiritual meaning of the Old Testament text; that is to say, their genre is commentary. But any reader of Bernard of Clairvaux's eighty-six sermons on the Song of Songs[53] knows that these commentaries are radically Christocentric texts. More to the point, they are powerful vehicles for describing the church's, and the individual believer's, intimate union with Jesus Christ. Bernard's sermons were very influential throughout the Middle Ages and continued to be influential among Protestant writers. In John Owen's *Of Communion with God the Father, Son, and Holy Ghost*, the long central section on communion with Christ takes the form of extended reflection on the Song of Songs.

Conclusion

This has been a rather scattershot survey of some historical experiments in genre, experiments driven by the structure of the doctrine of union with Christ. Theologians and spiritual writers are free in their choice of available genres, and are even free to concoct new genres that will be effective in their own eras and cultures. Surveying

---

53. See Bernard of Clairvaux, *On the Song of Songs*.

and comparing a range of options should have two effects: First, it should show that a vital soteriology of union with Christ has long been active in the Christian theological tradition and that we can see it clearly when we become alert to the sometimes unexpected genres in which it has been produced. But second, surveying the comparative options may also inspire current theologians to consider how the tradition can be carried forward in future works. Having rehearsed some of the options presented to us by the history of theology, we should maintain a lively sense of what we intend to accomplish when doing theological writing about union with Christ. What we seek is a doctrine of union with Christ that is obviously and resolutely about Christ, or that captures and enshrines the reality that salvation requires attention to Jesus Christ first, and only then moves to the way the reality of Jesus impacts or impinges on the life of the Christian. Our powers of attention need to be focused on the truth in Jesus more than on a biographical point in the life of the believer.

DOXOLOGICAL INTERLUDE

Three Unions (Polhill)

There are three admirable Unions noted by Divines; the essential Union of the Three persons in the Sacred Trinity; the Hypostatical Union of the divine and humane natures in the Person of Christ; and the Mystical Union which is between Christ and Believers.

In the first we have salvation in the primary fountain of it; in the second we have it in the channel or excellent medium of it; in the third we have it in the application or actual possession of it.

The Deity is an Immense Ocean of mercy and goodness, but it flows out to us only in and through a Mediator; Jesus Christ is a Mediator of Alsufficient righteousness and merit; but he communicates himself only to those that are in union with him.[1]

---

1. Polhill, *Christus in Corde*, unnumbered page of "Preface to the Christian Reader."

CHAPTER FOUR

Union with Christ as Trinitarian Soteriology

UNION WITH CHRIST is the classic Christian soteriological scheme and is closely linked with the doctrine of the Trinity, which is the classic Christian doctrine of God. The long lines of salvation reach all the way back through the incarnate Son to the triune God, and the entire history and order of salvation are suspended from the perfect fellowship of Father, Son, and Holy Spirit. In this chapter we will undertake a brief systematic account of union with Christ as the soteriology that fits best with an understanding of how the triune God brings about salvation.

The Order of Salvation

Genre matters, and one of this book's steady concerns has been to give proper attention to the genres of union-with-Christ soteriology. In chapter 2, it was the biblical genres themselves, the literary forms in which God as the author of Scripture presents to us the soteriology of union with Christ. First are the Gospels, accounts of the life of Christ narrated as inside stories and renarrated in the presence of the risen Lord in the power of the Holy Spirit. Secondly and supportively come the New Testament epistles, which rest on Jesus's life as they explain how our lives are saved in him. Chapter 3 began by noting how expositors like John Calvin drew out, by creative commentary, the narrative genre of union with Christ that was already enshrined in the creeds. The chapter concluded with a survey of some classic instances of writing out the truth of union with Christ in a way that directs our focus first of all to Jesus Christ himself and then annexes our salvation to him (examples like Thomas Aquinas's theology of the mysteries of the life of Christ, and Isaac Ambrose's meditative schema of *Looking unto Jesus*).

Having noted the theological resonance, richness, and abiding promise of these genres, we are now prepared to entertain a live question: Is the *ordo salutis* also an appropriate genre for writing the doctrine of union with Christ? Richard Muller defines *ordo salutis* as "the temporal order of causes and effects through which the salvation of the sinner is accomplished," noting that "the term *ordo salutis* itself is of late origin, usually thought to have originated in the early eighteenth century as the descriptor of the series of terms developed with reference to Romans 8:28–30 and Acts 26:17–18."[1] There is nothing necessarily Reformed about using the *ordo salutis* schema, and indeed it can be traced in Lutheran and Wesleyan settings, with predictably appropriate variations. But it is a genre most elaborately developed, and consistently evoked, in Reformed settings. Our question is, Is it a genre congenial to teaching union with Christ?

An *ordo*, after all, is a list rather than a narrative, and thus it moves in a different conceptual idiom than the other genres we have explored, including the main biblical genres themselves. The question about whether it is an appropriate genre is also not merely theoretical; it is a pointed question, because there have been thinkers who have answered in the negative, denying that an *ordo salutis* can contain or

---

1. Muller, *Dictionary of Latin and Greek Theological Terms*, 250.

even communicate the doctrine of union with Christ.[2] That contrast has been made in precisely this disjunctive form: you can either teach about union with Christ or you can teach about salvation according to an *ordo salutis*. Supposedly, on this account, the two worlds can never meet. But this mutual exclusivity view is a minority report, and an unnecessarily extreme one. While fully acknowledging the genre difference, we can also affirm that the doctrine of union with Christ can in fact be taught using the *ordo salutis* tradition and that this doctrine and this genre complement each other quite well. Union with Christ is bigger, stronger, more organic, more primal, and more inclined to rivet our attention on Jesus Christ himself than is the *ordo* tradition, but a well-explained order of salvation, even presented in chart format, can certainly play a valuable supporting role. There is no need to choose one over the other; a trinitarian soteriology of sufficient scope can easily accommodate both.

Let us begin by admitting the grain of truth in the criticism: union with Christ has never fit very snugly into the *ordo salutis*. We can call as our chief witness no less an advocate of the *ordo salutis* than John Murray, whose book *Redemption Accomplished and Applied* is probably the most influential popular-level presentation of the Reformed *ordo salutis*. Murray's book has fifteen chapters: five on atonement—that is, the titular "redemption accomplished"—and ten on the *ordo salutis*—that is, "redemption applied." Murray's survey explanation of the *ordo* begins with effectual calling and ends with glorification; in between he teaches about the other points of the *ordo*: regeneration, faith, justification, adoption, sanctification, and perseverance. Throughout, he makes a number of structural or systemic observations about why these elements should be ordered in this way. These systemic observations are probably one of the keys to his book's longevity and popularity, because they hold the presentation together wonderfully. Murray's Reformed commitments show up at several

---

2. For a well-documented report on some of these critics and a detailed refutation of their claims, see Fesko, "Romans 8.29–30 and the Question of the *Ordo Salutis*." Fesko's view is that "to talk about union with Christ is to discuss the *ordo* and vice-versa" (38).

points, not least in his arguments for why regeneration must precede faith (Wesleyans, of course, think the opposite: this apparently small inversion in the *ordo* is one of the best ways of grasping the difference between Reformed and Wesleyan accounts of soteriology). Murray devotes one chapter to our subject, union with Christ. So in that sense, the doctrine of union with Christ certainly fits into his *ordo salutis* book.

But the chapter on union with Christ is an unusual chapter within the structure of Murray's book. For one thing, he puts off his treatment of union with Christ as long as possible. He delays it until the penultimate chapter, the ninth chapter of ten in the "redemption applied" section of the book. The only thing that Murray treats later than union with Christ is the doctrine of glorification, which obviously has to come last because of its consummating character. So with that final spot reserved, Murray treats union with Christ as close to the end as possible. And as the end of the book draws near (page 161 out of 181), he gives solid reasons for saving it for last:

> Intelligent readers may have wondered why there has not been up to this point some treatment of union with Christ. Obviously it is an important aspect of the application of redemption and, if we did not take account of it, not only would our presentation of the application of redemption be defective but our view of the Christian life would be gravely distorted. Nothing is more central or basic than union and communion with Christ.[3]

Notice already the high estimation Murray has of the doctrine of union: "Nothing is more central or basic." So while it fits in the book and indeed *must* find a place in the book for its teaching to avoid being gravely distorted, it does not exactly fit inside the *ordo* itself; it is not co-*ord*inated with the *ordo*, as he points out (it is not clear to me whether Murray intends the wordplay on *ordo*). Murray explains:

3. Murray, *Redemption Accomplished and Applied*, 161.

Union with Christ as Trinitarian Soteriology

There is, however, a good reason why the subject of union with Christ should not be co-ordinated with the other phases of the application of redemption with which we have dealt. That reason is that union with Christ is in itself a very broad and embracive subject. It is not simply a step in the application of redemption; when viewed, according to the teaching of Scripture, in its broader aspects it underlies every step of the application of redemption. Union with Christ is really the central truth of the whole doctrine of salvation not only in its application but also in its once-for-all accomplishment in the finished work of Christ. Indeed the whole process of salvation has its origin in one phase of union with Christ and salvation has in view the realization of other phases of union with Christ. This can readily be seen if we remember that brief expression which is so common in the New Testament, namely, "in Christ." It is that which is meant by "in Christ" that we have in mind when we speak of "union with Christ." It is quite apparent that the Scripture applies the expression "in Christ" to much more than the application of redemption. A certain aspect of union with Christ, it is true, belongs strictly to the application of redemption. With that we shall deal later. But we would not deal properly with the subject of union with Christ unless we set forth, first of all, its broader meaning. We would not be able to appreciate that which falls within the application of redemption if we did not relate it to that which is broader.[4]

This is crucial to note: not only does union with Christ outflank and overwhelm the entire sequence of redemption's application, it even oversteps the boundary that distinguishes redemption accomplished from redemption applied. Think of the book's famous title: *Redemption Accomplished and Applied*. And yet one subject treated under the heading of "redemption applied" turns out to overarch the entire text: "Union with Christ is really the central truth of the whole doctrine of salvation not only in its application but also in its once-for-all accomplishment in the finished work of Christ." That is, even Christ's own accomplishment of his finished work, the act of

4. Murray, *Redemption Accomplished and Applied*, 161–62.

atonement proper, is itself an expression of the central truth, which is union with Christ.

This admission in chapter 14, twenty pages from the end of the book, really does threaten to challenge the book's entire founding idea, reaching all the way back to the distinction drawn in its title. Murray obviously believes that the *ordo salutis* and union with Christ belong together in one exposition, but it's easy to see why critics might mount a more radical critique. Union with Christ is so large that it overwhelms the *ordo* presentation and might threaten to destroy it. But even in the act of pointing out union's expansiveness, Murray maintains its compatibility with the *ordo* schema. He calls union with Christ "broad and embracive," not "broad and explosive." Theologians simply need to bear constantly in mind, as they work with the *ordo salutis*, that everything in it takes place inside of union with Christ, or even more simply, more obviously, and more biblically, *in* Christ.

Murray goes on to say that "union with Christ is a very inclusive subject. It embraces the wide span of salvation from its ultimate source in the eternal election of God to its final fruition in the glorification of the elect."[5] And then he repeats some of his previous ways of describing it:

> It is not simply a phase of the application of redemption; it underlies every aspect of redemption both in its accomplishment and in its application. Union with Christ binds all together and insures that to all for whom Christ has purchased redemption he effectively applies and communicates the same. But union with Christ is an important part of the application of redemption. We do not become actual partakers of Christ until redemption is effectually applied.[6]

Murray doesn't give much space to explaining the two different ways he is using the category of union with Christ, but it is clear

5. Murray, *Redemption Accomplished and Applied*, 165.
6. Murray, *Redemption Accomplished and Applied*, 165.

that he considers there to be two distinct ways. On the one hand, union is a reality larger than the entire *ordo salutis*, indeed larger than the accomplished-applied schema itself; and on the other hand, union is an entry point into the application of redemption. So it both encompasses the field and is a point of entry to one subfield. Murray admits the difficulty of having the union motif functioning at two levels, but he maintains the distinction because it comes close to doing justice to the fullness of the Bible's way of speaking.

Evidently it is possible to accept gratefully the *ordo salutis* as a teaching tool—that is, as a genre that helps support well-ordered teaching about union with Christ. The basic outlines of an *ordo* schema show up in Scripture (Rom. 8:29–30 and elsewhere). The *ordo* helpfully outlines the many facets of salvation and is especially well suited to the systematic task of clarifying the relations among those parts. The *ordo* schema excels at enabling us to make clear distinctions so that we can take the things distinguished conceptually and unite them in reality. But even John Murray recognizes that in some ways the *ordo* needs to be turned inside out—or opened up to transcendent referents—if it is going to be a hospitable home for the great theme of union with Christ. The house of *ordo* needs some new pictures on the wall, or a lot of mirrors inside to make sure the vital truths are reflected everywhere and distributed throughout the system. Better yet, it needs a vast skylight, down through which the transcendent truth of salvation can shine its undivided light to fall on each particular.

Union Accomplished: Contemplating Atonement

Murray's own recognition that union with Christ oversteps the distinction between salvation accomplished and salvation applied is one way of opening up that necessary skylight. Again, union with Christ is "the central truth of the whole doctrine of salvation not only in its application but also in its once-for-all accomplishment in the finished work of Christ."[7] In other words, even while Murray was spending five chapters under the heading of "redemption accomplished," discussing the necessity, nature, perfection, and extent of the atonement, he was implicitly moving in the sphere of union with Christ. What are we to make of this? Is union with Christ also a theory of the atonement? Do we need to assign it to two places: first to a position among the various theories of the atonement, and second to a place within the *ordo salutis*? We do not. In fact, the questions themselves, though they occur naturally and with the power of apparent self-evidence, are badly put.

Modern discussions of the atonement have long been in notable disarray, and it is a kind of disarray that is antithetical to the unified treatment of union with Christ we are pursuing. There is fragmentation in modern atonement theology that needs to be repaired before we can begin to understand union with Christ as embracively including both the accomplishment and the application of redemption. We began chapter 1 by insisting that there is such a thing as the one common Christian doctrine of salvation. The denial of that unity has taken on one particular form in the modern period, to which we need to pay close attention. Recall that J. N. D. Kelly contrasts patristic precision about Trinity and Christology with the comparative undefined and unfocused account of soteriology in early Christian theology. In his words, "Redemption did not become a battle-ground for rival schools until the twelfth century, when Anselm's *Cur deus homo* (c. 1097) focused attention on it."[8] Kelly says that the student of soteriology "must be prepared to pick his way through a variety of theories, to all appearance unrelated and even mutually incompatible, existing side by side and sometimes sponsored by the same theologian."[9] We have acknowledged the element of truth in this observation. But Kelly's language is telling. It gives away too much, and in fact it gives away Kelly's own location in the intellectual currents

---

7. Murray, *Redemption Accomplished and Applied*, 162.
8. Kelly, *Early Christian Doctrines*, 375.
9. Kelly, *Early Christian Doctrines*, 375.

Union with Christ as Trinitarian Soteriology

of the mid-twentieth century.[10] Kelly did excellent work in historical theology, and his two best books, *Early Christian Creeds* and *Early Christian Doctrines*, remain in print and can be used with great profit. But the idea that soteriology comes to us in the form of "a variety of theories, to all appearance unrelated and even mutually incompatible," is itself an idea with a late modern pedigree. Viewing the history of soteriology as something that doesn't start until Anselm's work and thereby establishing the possibility of "rival schools" by setting forth a systematic theory is a mistaken reading of the history based on a kind of category error. The fundamental error comes from conceiving of atonement theology as divided up into numerous theories. Whether this conception is true or not, believing it to be true is a relatively recent development.

In a far-reaching article,[11] Adam Johnson has traced the genealogy of this way of thinking, which began with the work of F. C. Baur on the history of dogma. Baur approached the history of doctrine as if it were made up of a sequence of competing systems that vied with each other for supremacy, developing across time in a dynamic process of growth through conflict. Baur's deeper reasons for construing the history of ideas this way were idealist and Hegelian, but his influence was not limited to intellectuals who shared his philosophical commitments. His influence was widespread. From about 1870 on, the novel category of "theories of the atonement" took hold, and almost everyone began "working with the historical material through the rubric of discrete competing 'theories' of the atonement—a vision which deeply shaped the work of proponents and opponents alike, and gave rise to a range of categories and nomenclatures which shape discussions to this day."[12] Johnson traces the history well, but anybody who has read an introductory text on atonement has almost certainly

---

10. Kelly lived from 1909 to 1997. His book *Early Christian Creeds* appeared in 1950 with a revised third edition in 1972. His *Early Christian Doctrines* appeared in 1958 with a fifth edition in 2000.

11. Johnson, "Theories and *Theoria* of the Atonement."

12. Johnson, "Theories and *Theoria* of the Atonement," 100.

taken in the influence of Baur's categories and can recite some version of the typology of atonement theories: ransom, satisfaction, penal substitution, *Christus victor*, and so on. In recent decades, there has been a growing consensus that a large number of flowers bloom in the garden of atonement, and the best we can do is pick a bouquet that makes the best of each variety of theory.[13]

There is some plausibility to this way of thinking about unity and variety in atonement theology. Various people have various opinions. But as a standard way of presenting the doctrine of the atonement, it is somewhat stodgy and standoffish. It has a tendency to make students feel immediately wiser than all previous theologians (who were evidently never so flexible in their way of thinking about the subject and never even knew that they were operating with theories). As a settled set of presuppositions, or as the new orthodoxy about atonement, it is historically misleading, and it systematically hobbles in advance the possibility of thinking large, integrative thoughts about soteriology. It is also worth noticing what a tempting framework it is; even as I step back from committing to it, I feel a desire to enter the fray and defend the vicarious punishment theory of atonement against its detractors. If there is a fight over which flower arrangement works best in the bouquet of atonement, it's hard not to take sides.[14]

But according to Johnson, the way of wisdom is to prescind from the whole project of gathering atonement nosegays.[15] Notice that formally speaking, the project puts the contemporary theologian far too much in charge of deciding what goes in, what stays out, and how it's arranged. Flower arrangement is a real art, and this modern method of composing atonement teaching puts the theologian in the position

---

13. A good sample of this way of arguing can be found, appropriately, in a four-views book. See Beilby and Eddy, *Nature of the Atonement*. Joel Green's presentation of a "kaleidoscopic view" (157–85) is especially clear and methodologically self-aware about working within the variety of options. Green states his own view more fully in Baker and Green, *Recovering the Scandal of the Cross*.

14. The blood of Christ is the red rose without which no bouquet is beautiful or adequate. But I make this point in a footnote, showing remarkable restraint.

15. For further discussion, see Johnson, *Atonement and the Life of Faith*, in this series.

of making all the difference. That is too much power for a theologian; something has gone wrong even if it comes out all right. Formally speaking, this theological method emphasizes individual choice and selection, which is *hairesis*, the Greek root of the word "heresy." The modern habit of teaching theories of atonement is not heresy, and its contents may in fact be highly orthodox. But it does embed selectivity in the very formal structure of inquiry and teaching. Since the beginning of this modern way of teaching atonement, its practitioners have often been spurred on to generate a kind of master account, or unified field theory, that comprehends all the others. Johnson quotes an early objector to this theories-of-atonement mode of working, who points out that Baur (and company) has a "passion for *systematizing*, which sometimes leads him to give exclusive or disproportionate value to one side of a writer's view, to the exclusion or neglect of others," and that his work has an "essentially negative cast, preternaturally alive to the slightest indications of inconsistency, while unable to recognize the plainest evidences of unity."[16] Imagine how such analysts read the great classics of Christian soteriology, forcing Athanasius, Aquinas, and Calvin to represent distinct theories, while systematically suppressing the constant notes of agreement, the "plainest evidences of unity." This is the genealogy of Kelly's fairly calm and unalarming remark that redemption has become "a battle-ground for rival schools" on which a student "must be prepared to pick his way through a variety of theories, to all appearance unrelated and even mutually incompatible, existing side by side and sometimes sponsored by the same theologian."[17] Even a commentator as fair-minded as Kelly has learned the modern habit of thinking that atonement theology is something that comes to us in theories. He has learned it so thoroughly that he refuses to drop it even when he has to admit that these theories are broadly distributed, sit "side by side," and were treated by earlier theologians as not mutually exclusive. Moderns are in the

16. Johnson, "Theories and *Theoria* of the Atonement," 103 (italics original).
17. Kelly, *Early Christian Doctrines*, 375.

strange position of using their nineteenth-century "theory analysis" to categorize thirteenth- and sixteenth-century authors as advocates of these distinct theories. But the texts of these earlier authors refuse to obey the nineteenth-century categories and insist on containing, as they always have, all sorts of ways of speaking of the atonement.

The way forward, as Johnson recommends, is not theories but *theoria*, the Greek word for contemplation. John Webster warns that "a good deal of modern theology has been reluctant to consider contemplation [*theoria*] a proper end of theological intelligence."[18] Johnson's extended paraphrase of Webster's observation is that "a good deal of modern theology has been reluctant to contemplate those treatises which would guide it into a fuller and more comprehensive understanding of the death and resurrection of Jesus, resting content with one-dimensional, reductionistic and therefore easily contrasted accounts of those works. The goal is not one of *wissenschaft* but *theoria*—first of God, and then of theological texts." In other words, "*theoria*, contemplation of God, particularly through God's saving work in Jesus Christ, is the governing paradigm for the pre-modern theological task"[19] and should also become our goal in the theology of the atonement. The goal will be clearer to us if, following Murray's insights, we recognize atonement as being already included within union with Christ, embracively considered.

Perhaps some readers may be concerned that Johnson's theories-versus-*theoria* dichotomy is too extreme. I can imagine teachers who find it pedagogically helpful to take students on a tour around the various theories, pointing out their respective internal logics, contrasting them with one another for clarity's sake, and then integrating them all into a synthesis of some sort. Perhaps the tour even concludes with an exhortation to remember that after all is said and done we are approaching a single atonement from this variety of perspectives. One might even go through the lecture notes and replace the

---

18. Webster, *God without Measure*, 1:220, cited in Johnson, "Theories and *Theoria* of the Atonement," 104. Bracketed word in Johnson's text.

19. Johnson, "Theories and *Theoria* of the Atonement," 106.

word "theories" with "facets" to keep up the suggestion of a massive unity behind the perplexity. Or one might reorient the doctrine around unity in a less superficial way, making the achievement of synthesis the primary goal.[20] Perhaps there is a way forward through the thicket of theories to a vista that doesn't lose the forest for the trees. But anyone who wants to keep thinking about atonement in "theories" should be sure to heed with some precision Johnson's four warnings about the schema on the basis of its recent origins. First, there is the danger of anachronism: "To speak of Calvin's or Irenaeus' 'theory' of the work of Christ is to employ a category they themselves did not use, and therefore to run the risk of interpreting their thought in ways alien to their own intentions."[21] Second, distortion: theory language presupposes "philosophical, epistemological or other commitments which distort the thought of those we seek to interpret." In particular, "theory language emerges from a context saturated with idealist presuppositions,"[22] an exotically modern lens to use on premodern theology. Third, teaching atonement using a "theories" conceptuality means inviting students to uncritically adopt a set of "distinctions and categories of others in summarizing the history of the doctrine of the atonement."[23] While truly great teachers may use these categories to deliver an effective and inspirational lecture on atonement, the more common result will be bland, potted summaries of the four or five (or however many) "main theories" from Aulén or Baur or their epigones. Fourth, the theories convention intentionally plays up conflict and difference; it was designed for the purpose of "parsing the history of the doctrine into different historically conditioned and mutually exclusive camps."[24] Those who use it are blinded to the long lines of continuity that run throughout the tradition, and the vast common reservoir

---

20. The most successful recent work along these lines is McNall, *Mosaic of Atonement*.
21. Johnson, "Theories and *Theoria* of the Atonement," 100.
22. Johnson, "Theories and *Theoria* of the Atonement," 101.
23. Johnson, "Theories and *Theoria* of the Atonement," 102.
24. Johnson, "Theories and *Theoria* of the Atonement," 103.

of soteriology that we would after all expect from generation after generation reading the same Bible.

What difference would it make to set union with Christ in its proper place over atonement theology? We have already seen how the whole redemption-applied field is in fact a way of itemizing and articulating the primal, holistic reality of union with Christ. Our grasp of atonement would similarly be changed by recognizing that the whole redemption-accomplished field is also under the banner of union with Christ. In one sense, we are arguing that union with Christ imparts theological unity to soteriology in both registers, accomplished and applied. But the cases are not fully parallel. On the redemption-applied side, theologians using the *ordo salutis* genre simply need to remain alert to its status as an analytic schema that helps in the exploration of the vast reality of union with Christ. But on the redemption-accomplished side, theologians in the habit of using the theories-of-atonement genre would be well advised to stop. It is a misleading schema based on pernicious presuppositions and should be replaced with serious work in which *theoria*, contemplation of Christ as the salvation of God, makes a difference in the way we teach and dispute. In both cases, soteriology needs to deploy the doctrine of union with Christ embracively, establishing a fundamental unity and simplicity across the full range of soteriology.

Kevin Vanhoozer has referred to something he calls "the *simplicity* of union" with Christ. He draws out the meaning by analogy:

> In brief: union is to soteriology what the doctrine of divine simplicity is to theology proper. The doctrine of divine simplicity states that God is not a composite of his parts; rather, his being is coextensive with his attributes. For example, God does not "have" love; God is love. And now to the analogy: just as God is one, so salvation is simple. In the words of Richard Gaffin: "There is but one union, with distinguishable but inseparable, coexisting legal and renovative aspects."[25]

25. Vanhoozer, "From 'Blessed in Christ' to 'Being in Christ,'" 10–11. Vanhoozer's quotation of Gaffin is from Gaffin, *By Faith, Not by Sight*, 43.

While we have been treating union with Christ as something so comprehensive and complex that it verges on totality, Vanhoozer proposes treating it as soteriologically simple. It contains so much, and contains it all so irreducibly and inseparably, that it must be a single, definite something with its own integrity and gestalt. This would explain why it fits everywhere and nowhere in the *ordo salutis*, why it calls for the sort of contemplative reception that Johnson calls *theoria* rather than dissection into theories, and why it outflanks the accomplished-applied distinction. Vanhoozer explains further that "just as each divine attribute gives us a perspective on God's being, so each element in the order of salvation—not only justification and sanctification but election, and glorification as well—shines a light on another aspect of our union with Christ."[26]

In a sense, we are of course calling for a larger perspective on union with Christ. But it bears repeating that this proposed larger perspective is not a radical revision of traditional categories; it does not deconstruct them or even relativize the fairly standard Protestant account of union. In particular, as we undertake to bring union with Christ together with the *ordo salutis* schema, we should bear steadily in mind that we are not departing from predictable Protestant sources but merely making sure to take seriously what Protestants themselves have consistently claimed about union. As Sinclair Ferguson argues, "Every element in the classical *ordo salutis* is thus a further perspective on the one reality of the believer's union with Christ."[27] Our star witness in this respect has been John Murray, and we would do well to return to him and notice that in his book on the *ordo salutis* he concludes his sweeping chapter on union with Christ with two important gestures toward an expansive vista on the doctrine.

Murray's first gesture is toward the mystical element of the mystic union: "Union with Christ is mystical because it is a mystery. The fact that it is a mystery underlines the preciousness of it and the intimacy

---

26. Vanhoozer, "From 'Blessed in Christ' to 'Being in Christ,'" 11.
27. Ferguson, *Holy Spirit*, 106, quoted in Vanhoozer, "From 'Blessed in Christ' to 'Being in Christ,'" 11.

of the relation it entails."[28] He of course reserves the right to guard the word "mysticism" against excesses and misunderstandings, but he insists on using it in its correct sense: "It is necessary for us to recognize that there is an intelligent mysticism in the life of faith."[29] By way of proof Murray glances over "the wide range of similitude used in Scripture to illustrate union with Christ."[30] This is a strategic maneuver we will see below in Edward Polhill; it is the standard way of casting a wide net over Scripture's way of talking about this central mystery. The conclusion Murray draws is that our union with Christ cannot be reduced to something as low and naturalistic as a backward glance at salvation, as if it were merely located in the distant past of salvation history. Instead, the doctrine describes something personal and present:

> Believers are called into the fellowship of Christ and fellowship means communion. The life of faith is one of living union and communion with the exalted and ever-present Redeemer. Faith is directed not only to a Redeemer who has come and completed once for all a work of redemption. It is direct to him not merely as the one who died but as the one who rose again and who ever lives as our great high priest and advocate.[31]

Murray's second gesture toward the bigger picture is to indicate the trinitarian character of the mystery. This character of the mystery, he tells us, "must not be omitted," for "if it were overlooked there would be a serious defect in our understanding and appreciation of the implications of this union."[32] Definite trinitarian implications "arise from the relations of Christ to the other persons of the trinity and from our relations to the other persons of the trinity by reason of

28. Murray, *Redemption Accomplished and Applied*, 167.
29. Murray, *Redemption Accomplished and Applied*, 169.
30. Murray, *Redemption Accomplished and Applied*, 167–68.
31. Murray, *Redemption Accomplished and Applied*, 169.
32. Murray, *Redemption Accomplished and Applied*, 172.

our union with Christ."[33] Those who have union with Christ also have a kind of union with the Father, with whom Christ the Son is strongly unified. The Father and Son together, as Jesus says in one remarkable passage, will come to the believer who loves Jesus and keeps his word: "We will come to him and make our home with him" (John 14:23). The Spirit likewise, in a series of Jesus's statements, is promised as a divine presence to those who belong to Jesus (John 14:16–17). As Murray summarizes the trinitarian range of this mystery: "It is union, therefore, with the Father and with the Son and with the Holy Spirit that union with Christ draws along with it."[34] All of this, I emphasize, is in the standard, popular, evangelical Protestant reference works on union with Christ. Union with Christ is widely recognized as the best way into fully trinitarian soteriology.

Three Mysteries of Union

There are three great mysteries in Christian theology: the Trinity, the incarnation, and union with Christ. These three mysteries are all mysteries of unity. The mystery of the Trinity is how the three persons (Father, Son, and Holy Spirit) are the one, only God. The mystery of the incarnation is how the divine nature is united to human nature in the person of our one Lord, Jesus Christ. And the mystery of union with Christ is how the believers are joined to Christ to participate in the salvation he accomplishes.

These three mysteries are mega-doctrines, large clusters of theological truth that draw together data from all over the Bible. They are each comprehensively large, too large to locate all in one place, which is why they are represented doctrinally by words that aren't directly biblical. The Bible says, "The Word became flesh," but the noun formation "incarnation" is a conceptual tool for gathering that statement about the Word becoming flesh (John 1:14) and combining it

---

33. Murray, *Redemption Accomplished and Applied*, 171.
34. Murray, *Redemption Accomplished and Applied*, 172.

with all the other biblical testimony to who Jesus Christ is. The word "Trinity" is likewise an extrabiblical word for a biblical idea, an idea so expansive that you have to take a step back and see the Bible as a whole to take it all in. Union with Christ, meanwhile, is most nearly a directly biblical way of speaking. But as a comprehensive doctrine of salvation, it takes on a special scope and range.

The tradition of grouping these three mysteries together, as we have just done, is a rhetorical and pedagogical maneuver designed to join up soteriology with the great realities in which it participates and from which it derives its meaning. This three-mysteries approach reminds the audience, before they take up the topic of salvation itself, that there is a larger horizon of Christian truth behind the experience of salvation. The order is perfect: God the Trinity, Christ the incarnate one, and then salvation. The first mystery is infinitely the highest and greatest of all unions. Three persons existing as one God, having the one numerically same essence, mutually indwelling one another and acting inseparably with one energy. That indestructible, incorruptible oneness is the source of the other unities. The Son carries divine unity into his incarnate existence, assuming human nature into personal union with himself with no confusion or division, no mixing or separating. Our union with Christ depends especially on that hypostatic union. Viewed from above, our union with Christ is the nearest edge of an integrated series, a cascading reality of unions and unifications, onenesses flowing downward from the one God to heal our divisions and disintegrations.

The three-mysteries gambit leads the student's mind away from a too narrow consideration of salvation and takes them on an itinerary into the depths of God. It can be a short trip, a mere gesture at the infinite horizon, a suggestion that something much greater is out there, communicating its own very determinate meaning and purposes. But it reminds us all that salvation is not a topic that can just be picked up and handled on its own terms. The Christian doctrine of salvation takes all its orders from prior considerations about who does the saving (the triune God) and what resources must be mobilized to provide for the gospel (the presence of the God-man). Edward Polhill provides a classic statement of it: "There are three admirable Unions: (1) The essential union of three persons in the Sacred Trinity—These three are one (1 John 5:7), that is, one in essence. (2) The hypostatical Union of the Divine and Humane natures in the person of Christ; . . . (3) The mystical union which is between Christ and his Church."[35] Polhill focuses on the centrality of Christ in the entire nexus of mysteries: "Touching these three unions, an Ancient hath observed, That all three may be seen in Christ; he hath a Father (I may add, and a Spirit) with whom he is one substance; he hath an humane nature, with which he is one person; he hath adhering Believers, with whom he is one Spirit."[36]

A great nineteenth-century spiritual writer, Adolph Saphir (1831–91), takes up the same "three unions" tradition, lovingly tracing the way that Trinity and incarnation are perfections of unity before turning to "the union, which, according to the will of the Father, subsists between Christ and the Church."[37] Saphir draws this application of viewing the three unions together:

> We believe these unions, though we cannot comprehend and fathom them. We have a knowledge and experience of these mysteries in our hearts and lives, an assurance and consolation continually flowing from these eternal depths, and we wait with calmness and hope for the bright and perfect knowledge which shall be ours when we see face to face. Eternity alone can unfold the blessedness of those who know "the name of the Father, and of the Son, and of the Holy Ghost."[38]

35. Polhill, *Christus in Corde*, 9. Polhill repeats some of this formula from his own "Preface to the Christian Reader," nine pages earlier in the book. I quoted from that preface version in the doxological interlude before this chapter. In quoting this version from page 9 of *Christus in Corde*, I have made some changes in the erratic punctuation and added the numbering.

36. Polhill, *Christus in Corde*, 9–10. The "Ancient" Polhill cites is Bernard of Clairvaux, as he tells his readers in a marginal note.

37. Saphir, *Christ and the Church*, 87.

38. Saphir, *Christ and the Church*, 88.

Saphir is free to begin with the incarnation, move backward to the Trinity, and then conclude with union with Christ. The three-unions schema makes this possible. Whatever part of the nexus of mysteries teachers draw attention to, if they do it using the three-mysteries framework, they are recognizably following the same pedagogical strategy of putting salvation into its trinitarian-christological context.

Every pedagogical schema involves trade-offs, and a possible weakness of the three-unions schema can be seen in the way it relativizes the accomplishment of atonement. In fact, we might imagine teaching four unions, beginning with the Trinity and the incarnation, then proceeding through the atonement (the mystery of reconciliation), and only then union with Christ (the mystery of fellowship). That four-beat story of mysterious unions would have the advantage of putting the doctrine of God and the doctrine of incarnation at the foundation of redemption accomplished and then applied. Redemption accomplished ought to be centered on the cross, while redemption applied ought to shift our attention to the experiential phase of union with Christ. Saphir's way of teaching the three unions nearly jumps over salvation accomplished and goes straight to salvation applied. In doing so, Saphir runs the risk of de-emphasizing the cross, or of hurrying past it in an unseemly way. But if we read more charitably (especially in light of his other writings on the death of Christ), it is possible to see him as presupposing the atoning death as the foundation of the mystical union whose praises he goes on to sing. By turning his attention to union with Christ rather than to the atonement, Saphir is going further into the heart of the whole doctrine of salvation. He is furthermore gaining the advantage of highlighting the unification brought about, which is the union or oneness between Christ and his church. Emphasizing atonement is a way of highlighting the great estrangement that had to be overcome to make this union possible, an estrangement that was not an issue in the unions of the Trinity or the incarnation. Elevating atonement to a place within the three-unions schema would be jarring because it would introduce this dramatic moment of conflict and reversal.

We would have to go from trinitarian theology proper, wherein no conflict or estrangement is to be found, by way of incarnation, which involves contrast but no conflict, to the cross, which is the focus of the greatest divine-human contradiction and resolution. Union with Christ, on the other hand, presupposes the completed atonement but dwells on an experience of unity. Trinity, incarnation, and union with Christ are three mysteries of union that hang together more fittingly. Emphasizing union with Christ is a way of highlighting the depth of the unity achieved by salvation.

Christ-Centered and Trinity-Centered

Having made the trinitarian background and setting of salvation more explicit, we are prepared to take up an abiding problematic in Christian soteriology. There is a perceived difficulty in maintaining a concrete, definite focus on Jesus Christ as the center of salvation while also undistractedly recognizing the presence of God the Father and God the Holy Spirit in the same work. There is a felt tension, in other words, between soteriology's Christocentric impulse, on the one hand, and its trinitarian impulse, on the other. This tension continues to be felt even among evangelical theologians who know there can be no real contradiction between the two. It is a tension that also registers troublingly in the spirituality of ordinary believers.

Because of this felt tension, it is worthwhile to draw out and consider some of the ways in which union with Christ is trinitarian. The doctrine of union with Christ certainly seems to be a Christocentric soteriology, and yet it thrives and flourishes in an elaborately trinitarian setting.

There are, of course, vital polemical reasons for bringing these two doctrines closer together. Certain explicitly nontrinitarian theological systems attempt to appeal to union with Christ as their soteriological mechanism. Think of the unorthodox but very Jesus-centered theologies of modalist and subordinationist groups: Oneness Pentecostalism, on the one hand, or Arian and Socinian theologies, on the other hand. In those contexts, it would be worthwhile to demonstrate that the soteriology of union with Christ depends on the theology proper of the Trinity, without which it ceases to function or to signify salvation. But this book does not argue at that level. The goal of our instruction is Christian confidence in the coherence of the doctrine of union with Christ with the doctrine of the Trinity. So we will be seeking resonances and mutual illuminations between being in Christ and believing in the Trinity. There are many, and they matter.

When people ask whether our thinking should be Christ-centered or Trinity-centered, the obvious reply is to reject the false dichotomy being offered. To accept the possibility that these are two different centers is to give the whole game away before the first play. If Christ and the Trinity are separate centers, they can only be related elliptically, or *ec*centrically. But they are instead *con*centric. The best way to demonstrate this is to begin with the Christocentric impulse and to ask what that center is centered on. If Christ is the center, what is his center? This concentric approach is appropriate for two reasons.

First, it acknowledges that there is something utterly obvious, correct, and healthy about the Christian instinct to focus on Christ. To approach the nexus of saving mysteries concentrically is to honor the Christocentric impulse fully. Of course we start with him. And we especially start with him and focus on him when our whole approach to salvation is by way of the doctrine of union with Christ. The apostle Paul leads us by the hand in Ephesians to see salvation "in Christ," repeating this key phrase over and over, riveting our attention on salvation as inclusion in Christ: "Even when we were dead in our trespasses, [God] made us alive together with Christ—by grace you have been saved—and raised us up with him and seated us with him in the heavenly places in Christ Jesus" (Eph. 2:5–6). This Christocentric impulse is fundamentally right, and rightly fundamental. The Christian mind could not fully rest in any system that advises it to be only partly Christ-centered in its soteriology and to save some attention for other factors. Treating Trinity and Christology concentrically lets us direct all our faith, hope, and love toward one central truth. Our grasp of salvation is surest when it is most centered on Christ, when we look to him for "our whole salvation and all its parts."[39]

But the second reason that it is good to think concentrically is that it draws us deeper into the infinite resources that constitute Jesus Christ as who he is. It makes sense that a soteriology of being in Christ would not be able to settle for a merely external account of what Jesus did or how Jesus saves, but would inevitably be drawn further into the interior secret of Jesus's own identity. What is that secret? The Father knows it. Indeed, no one knows the Son except the Father (Matt. 11:27). Jesus is who he is, says what he says, and does what he does because of the Father who sent him. The doctrine of soteriology nests into Christology, and Christology shows itself to be fundamentally about the Son of the Father. To make the interpersonal communion fully trinitarian, we will of course want to name explicitly the Third Person, the Holy Spirit (Matt. 28:19). Christology nests into trinitarianism because Jesus is who he is as a person of the Trinity.

Let us restate this in terms of doctrinal order. We start our doctrine of union with Christ conceptually by placing Christ at the center of it and then inquiring about Christ's own center. When we realize that his center is the Father, we recognize that in terms of good doctrinal order, we must in fact approach soteriology from the doctrine of God. The Father sends the Son to save in salvation history because the Father eternally begot the Son. It is because of the Son's eternal generation within the Godhead that he is the one sent forth to save. "When the fullness of time had come, God sent forth his Son, born of woman, born under the law, to redeem those who were under the law" (Gal. 4:4–5). John Webster observes that "an account of the missions or external acts of the Son of God will be preceded by an account of the divine processions which is their vital principle."[40] Or, "Formally expressed: a divine mission includes within itself and

---

39. See chap. 3 above, on Calvin, *Institutes of the Christian Religion* II.16.19, 527–28.
40. Webster, *God without Measure*, 1:50.

refers to an eternal procession by which the identity of its agent is constituted."[41] Even more directly we could say that the Son is sent from the Father because he eternally subsists from the Father. The filial character of his work flows from the filial character of his being with the Father, in the Spirit.

This leads us to a fuller understanding of trinitarian agency. Salvation in Christ is a divine work, and therefore a work of the triune God, or, as we might say, of "the whole Trinity." Thomas Goodwin considers the divine agency behind the justification of the ungodly in an especially penetrating way: "As Christ is the object of faith, so, when any soul is converted, and drawn to believe on him, there is the concurrence of all the three persons in the Trinity to that work, and that they all put forth conjointly a renewed act of agreement in it."[42] The trinitarian agency lying behind the work of justification by faith is not, for Goodwin, just one feature among many that might be explored. It is instead essential. He considers it "a subject of great and weighty moment" that "will be of use to you many ways to quicken your hearts." Here is how he expounds justification trinitarianly:

> When God doth convert and draw our souls on to believe, we use to look upon the work itself as a great work wrought in ourselves. . . . But there is more done for us in heaven than is done in our hearts at that time. At that great union which is made between Christ and the soul, and the drawing on of the heart to close with Christ, there is a special council called; there is a concurrence, a consent, a joint meeting of all three persons to this great work, and that in a special manner. Though they concur in all works, yet where a council of them

41. Webster, *God without Measure*, 1:50.

42. Goodwin, *Object and Acts of Justifying Faith*, 144. There is some slippage here as I am engaging Goodwin to explain the trinitarian character of union with Christ, but mainly by drawing on his book about justification. The underlying grammar of divine action in soteriology is the same; Goodwin just happens to have made that grammar more explicit and thematic when writing about justification. For a full account of Goodwin on union with Christ, see Carter, *Thomas Goodwin on Union with Christ*.

Union with Christ as Trinitarian Soteriology

115

all is professedly called, there is a plain note and character of a more special and remarkable concurrence.[43]

How do the three persons do this work? There are traditional answers, and Goodwin is eager to expound them here in terms of a covenant of redemption. But the first thing to notice about salvation is that it is a work, an external action of the Trinity. Salvation is therefore, like all external actions of the Trinity, an undivided action of the entire Trinity. It can be understood in the same way as the incarnation itself: the whole Trinity brings about the incarnation, but only the Son takes human nature into hypostatic union with his own hypostasis as its terminus. Similarly, the whole Trinity brings about justification, or union with Christ. Yet it is only Christ to whom we are united.

Recall that "union with Christ" is the umbrella term covering both our inclusion in Christ and his indwelling in us. Formally, these seem like opposites: Is A in B, or is B in A? But Scripture guides us to understand both ways as describing the union between Christ and believers. So we can consider this union as a work of the Trinity in two ways: the Trinity places us in Christ, and the Trinity places Christ in us. Both actions originate from the Father and are perfected in the Spirit, but both center on the Son specifically as the incarnate one sent to take up our nature and unite us to himself.

A Brief Taxonomy of Trinitarian Action

Having glimpsed from a distance the way trinitarian action accounts for union with Christ, we are obligated to draw a little bit closer, to see some more detail. Let us rehearse the traditional taxonomy of trinitarian action, or at least those elements of it that contribute to union with Christ. We will proceed in three steps. First come some trinitarian categories proper. Basically, we start with the relations of origin, which describe how the persons of the Trinity exist with

43. Goodwin, *Object and Acts of Justifying Faith*, 144.

relation to one another. Second, we note that a certain kind of order is established by those relations of origin, which lets us say something meaningful about how they relate. Third, we can see that they work in a way that corresponds to how they exist and are ordered. We move from their processions, to their order, to their work. To do so we will call on help from one of the most clear and concise Protestant theologians of all time, Petrus van Mastricht (1630–1706). The distinctions he makes are not his own inventions, but his account of them is especially helpful. His taxonomy is just elaborate enough to stick well in the mind. In his reflections on the Trinity, Mastricht is so committed to divine unity that he recognizes how hard it is to distinguish among these three persons who possess the very same divine nature. So he poses the question, How do the three persons differ among themselves?[44] And he gives three answers, closely related and carefully sequenced.

First, Mastricht says, the three persons differ in their hypostatic properties, or their manner of subsisting.[45] Notice how careful we must be with the word "properties," since we habitually think of properties as belonging to a nature. The three persons have the very same single nature, so any property of that nature belongs to each and all of them: co-everything. By saying they differ in "hypostatic properties," Mastricht is specifying that there is something about who they are rather than what they are that distinguishes them. They differ not in essence but in their persons (hypostases). The distinction between them, predictably, is in their relations of origin. The Father subsists with no relation of origin from any other person; his hypostatic manner of subsisting is to be himself from no other. The Son is eternally begotten, so we can describe his hypostatic manner of subsisting as being from the Father. And the Holy Spirit proceeds from the Father of the Son, taking his hypostatic manner of subsisting from both.

---

44. Mastricht, *Theoretical-Practical Theology*, 2:504.
45. Mastricht, *Theoretical-Practical Theology*, 2:504.

Union with Christ as Trinitarian Soteriology   117

This distinction in their manner of subsisting gives rise to the second way they differ: in their order of subsisting. *Manner* of subsisting grounds *order* of subsisting.[46] All this means is that the Father is the first person (subsisting from himself), the Son second (as from the Father), and the Spirit third (subsisting from the Father of the Son, and therefore being of them both). If it seems like all Mastricht is doing here is conceptually unpacking the relations of origin, that's because that's all he's doing. In fact, you can draw a straight line from the biblically revealed names "Father," "Son," and "Spirit," through the relations of begetting, being begotten, and being spirated, to the order of first, second, and third. No new data is being snuck in; categories are being refined and extended to provide a more spacious arena for theological understanding.

This first-second-third order gives rise, finally, to their mode of operating. Their mode of operating "imitates the manner of subsisting and of order, insofar as, outside himself, the Father works from himself, through the Son and the Holy Spirit; the Son from the Father, through the Holy Spirit; and the Holy Spirit from the Father and the Son, through himself."[47] These modes of operating could be described in a variety of ways. Mastricht seems especially fond of noting which person operates through which other: the Father through both others, the Son through the Spirit, the Spirit through himself. But he also rings the changes on which person each works from: the Father from himself, the Son from the Father, the Spirit from both. An alternative way of stating this trinitarian mode of operating is "from the Father, through the Son, in the Spirit." Gregory of Nyssa puts it this way: "Every operation . . . has its origin from the Father, and proceeds through the Son, and is perfected in the Holy Spirit."[48] The one God does all things in this unified from-through-in way.

The movement of thought that Mastricht follows is significant: first the manner of subsisting, from which follows an order of

46. Mastricht, *Theoretical-Practical Theology*, 2:504–5.
47. Mastricht, *Theoretical-Practical Theology*, 2:505.
48. Gregory of Nyssa, *On "Not Three Gods,"* 334.

subsisting, which together set the pattern for the mode of operating. It is crucial that the movement of thought begins with the relations of origin. In fact, our doctrinal desire to distinguish the persons from one another ought to be, as Mastricht's is, entirely satisfied by appeal to these relations of origin: the Son is the Son because of generation; the Spirit is the Spirit because of spiration. As Mastricht continues to trace the work of the Trinity outward to creatures, he is not hoping to discover in that outer work some fuller or better explanations of how they differ. To the contrary, he is bringing all these distinctions with him from the internal life of the Trinity into the external operations of God. The manner of subsisting (relations of origin) grounds the order of subsisting (first, second, third) and is reflected in the mode of operating (from, through, in). The primal perfection of the triune God's life in himself is graciously made present to us in God's free fellowship with us. We might say that a theologian like Mastricht is in the business of applying: applying the doctrine of the Trinity's eternal order to the analysis of the Trinity's temporal work.

This is the right way to think through the issues. When we consider the Trinity as causing our union with Christ, we are well equipped if we have this whole sweeping movement of thought in mind: from relations of origin, to order of subsisting, to order of working. The main reason is that this movement of thought enables us to confess that the work of the Trinity in uniting us to Christ is the undivided work of the entire Trinity, and yet the distinctions of the persons are preserved even in the undivided act. How so? Without an articulated account of how trinitarian action is grounded in the inner triune life, we would be tempted to find the distinctions in the outer work itself. We might, for example, subdivide the work and assign one-third of it to each person. Perhaps the Father opens our soul, the Son enters it, and the Spirit closes it up again. Perhaps the Father starts the union, the Son does most of it, and the Spirit completes it. But this way of thinking of union with Christ is precisely failing to contemplate it as undivided. As a consequence, we will always find ourselves drifting back toward thinking in terms of a dichotomy or a split focus between being Christ-centered and Trinity-centered. A reasonably well-developed taxonomy of trinitarian action enables us to be wholeheartedly Trinity-centered in the very act of focusing on Christ, since we have an intelligent grasp of how perfectly embedded the Son is in the full divine life of the Trinity. We know that "the Father does all things through the Word and in the Holy Spirit" and that this includes union with Christ; "in this way is the unity of the Holy Trinity preserved."[49]

Union with Christ is a union from the Father who sends, through the Son who is sent, completed in the Holy Spirit who is from the Father and from the Son. Salvation by union with Christ is an undivided act of the triune God, in which the three persons indivisibly act in a from-through-in structure that echoes or enacts their eternal relations. That triune action is the vehicle for the mission of the Son and the Spirit, by which they are personally present to us from the Father. Union with Christ describes our union with the Second Person, but the act of our being united to Christ is an act that comes from the Father, through the Son, in the Spirit.

The result is that we can look higher. Goodwin informs us that in salvation "there is more done for us in heaven than is done in our hearts."[50] One of the chief benefits of a trinitarian union-with-Christ soteriology is that it helps us glimpse salvation as not just the resolution of creaturely problems but as participation in the divine life. We are, of course, sinful creatures who need our maker to be our redeemer, to radically reorder our existence and resolve our creaturely problems. But there is more going on above than reordering, something going on "in heaven." As Goodwin says:

> Thou hast considerations what was done upon earth in thy own heart; but look up higher, and consider what was done in heaven as the original of all, and let that be the thing for which thou praisest and

---

49. Athanasius of Alexandria, *Letters to Serapion* 1.28.2–3, in Athanasius the Great and Didymus the Blind, *Works on the Spirit*, 97.

50. Goodwin, *Object and Acts of Justifying Faith*, 144.

blessest God. Go home, and down upon thy knees, and thank these three persons that have done all this for thee, though thou sawest it not, when thy heart was first drawn to Christ.[51]

We began by noting the abiding problem in soteriology of maintaining a concrete, definite focus on Jesus Christ as the center of salvation while also undistractedly recognizing the presence of God the Father and God the Holy Spirit in the same work. Note that this tension is most keenly felt among those who are less classically trinitarian in their operating assumptions about God. Thinking through soteriology at a high level requires some practice in grasping the works of the Trinity as inseparable operations.

With this trinitarian framework in place, certain elements of the doctrine of union with Christ emerge as more effortlessly prominent. Among these elements are the personal identity of Jesus Christ as one of the Trinity, the way union with Christ functions as an immersion into the full relational network of the life of the living God, and the admission of Jesus's entire ministry—all the mysteries of his life and "the whole course of his obedience"[52]—as the content of the doctrine of union. Confession of our status "in Christ" only thrives when it is located "in the Trinity."

51. Goodwin, *Object and Acts of Justifying Faith*, 151–52.
52. Calvin, *Institutes of the Christian Religion* II.16.5, 507.

DOXOLOGICAL INTERLUDE

"I Cannot Nearer Be" (Bonar)

So near, so very near to God,
I cannot nearer be;
For in the person of His Son,
I am as near as He.

So dear, so very dear to God,
More dear I cannot be;
The love wherewith He loves the Son,
Such is His love to me.[1]

---

1. These nineteenth-century hymn stanzas are of uncertain origin but are often attributed to either Horatius Bonar or Catesby Paget. For my best attempt to sort it out, see https://fredfredfred.com/2023/05/i-cannot-nearer-be/.

CHAPTER FIVE

Union with Christ and the Christian Life

THERE IS A WONDERFUL VARIETY to the lives lived by all the different kinds of followers of Christ. Discipleship has never been reducible to anything like a straightforward imitation, and certainly not to conformity to the particular details of Jesus's own vocation, culture, social location, fashion, diet, or mannerisms. To someone unfamiliar with the term, "Christlike" might suggest that sort of conformity, but in fact it has an altogether different meaning.

Still, for all the diversity we see among Christians around the world and across the ages, an underlying pattern nevertheless marks them out. If salvation is union with Christ, we would expect some kind of identifying unity among those united to him. That unity might be mysterious in a way that answers to the "mystic" element in the mystic union, but it is nevertheless real. Union with Christ does impart a consistent form to Christian experience, as believers are formed within the frame of Christ's own being. Put as simply and schematically as possible, that consistent form is a descent and ascent, a dying and rising to true life. The church indicates this externally in perpetual reenactment of the central ordinances of baptism and the

Lord's Supper. Baptism shows our being in Christ; the Lord's Supper shows Christ being in us.

This pattern takes its shape from the filial life of Christ the Son, who worked it out in person in his own incarnation, death, and resurrection. What he did for us and our salvation imparts its very own shape to us and our salvation. The long arc of his effective grace, reaching down and then taking up, is replicated in Christian experience. In this chapter, we first dwell on the way that pattern is established in Christ and then propagated to those who are in Christ; then we examine the transformed life that takes shape in believers.

Salvation Deposited and Dispensed (Zanchi)

In previous chapters we have explored the structure of salvation using the schema of redemption accomplished and applied. We found this schema to be a sturdy and capacious dual structure, crucial to the scope and integrity of soteriology. It focuses attention on Christ's objective work before turning attention to the subjective effect of that work on the recipient. It is strikingly Christ-centered in the way it portrays salvation as something with its own reality outside of us, in which we must come to participate by being joined up to it. But it retains this Christocentrism precisely by expanding the sphere of activity to the entire Trinity's appropriated works: the Father placing salvation in Christ, and the Spirit applying it to the believer. It makes room for a well-elaborated *ordo salutis* stretching from justification through glorification. The accomplished-applied schema, carefully inhabited, is a fitting venue in which to combine an emphasis on union with Christ with an articulation of an *ordo salutis*, while also recognizing that union itself is such a comprehensive motif that it can't be simply located at one spot on that *ordo*. We are not abandoning this trusty organizing principle. But there is at least one variation on this theme, or further specification of it, that helpfully highlights the next step we need to take in considering the Christian life.

Considered in terms of union with Christ, these two moments (salvation accomplished and applied) can also be seen as salvation first deposited in Christ, and then dispensed to believers. That deposited-dispensed schema emphasizes the riches of salvation in Christ and the way those riches flow out to the faithful. The theologian who has done the most with this schema is Girolamo Zanchi (1516–90), in the twelfth chapter of his *Confession of Christian Religion*.[1] Zanchi entitles that section "Of the True Dispensation of the Redemption," which evokes the great word *oikonomia*, the word used in Ephesians 1:10 to describe God's wise ordering of the comprehensive plan of salvation. The full title of Zanchi's *Confession*, chapter 12, is "Of the True Dispensation of the Redemption, the Salvation, and Life Which Is Laid Up in Christ Alone: And Therefore of the Necessary Uniting, and Participation with Christ."[2] It is because there is so much "laid up in Christ" (redemption, salvation, life) that "uniting and participating" with him is necessary. After his fulsome chapter title, Zanchi states his point in a more direct proposition: "Salvation and eternal life is laid in Christ, that from him it may be communicated to us."[3]

Zanchi's vision here begins with God the Son assuming human nature into union with himself and working out redemption in it. The incarnate one is righteous, is utterly conformed to God, and lives a life that both manifests an eternal quality and merits an eternal reward. The key point is that what Christ works out in himself is already, by intention and purpose, for us:

> The righteousness of Christ and the eternal life due unto him is not held in Christ alone, but is derived into all those, who by the regeneration of the Holy Spirit are made one with him and as true members

1. Zanchi, *De religione christiana fides / Confession of Christian Religion*, edited by Luca Baschera and Christian Moser (Brill, 2007). This Brill edition is a republishing of the 1599 English translation of the 1585 original; I have modernized the spelling and orthography. Later writers refer to this work briefly sometimes as the *Confession*, sometimes as *On Religion*.

2. Zanchi, *Confession*, 231.

3. Zanchi, *Confession*, 231. I have corrected the old translation here, which rendered *ut inde nobis communicetur* as "be communicated to be" rather than "be communicated to us."

are joined unto him as head of the whole church, and that to this end and purpose Christ came in the flesh, and that all our salvation and life consists in him, as in our head, that it may indeed be bestowed and communicated upon all the elect of God which are united unto him.[4]

Precisely because everything in the economy of salvation is oriented in advance toward us, we must come to participate in it:

> For even as the branch can draw no lively sap from the vine (John 15:1–7), nor the bough from the tree, nor the members any motion, sense, or life from the head, unless they be joined to the vine and tree and these to the head; even so cannot men receive any salvation or life from Christ (in whom only it consists), unless they be grafted into him and coupled in a true and real union, and being coupled, do abide in him.[5]

The prevenience of Christ's action is crucial here, and in expounding it, Zanchi opens up the category of union to reveal that there are in fact multiple unions to be distinguished within it. Though he is pressing for his readers to pursue union with Christ by participation in the life of Christ, Zanchi begins further back with an account of Christ's initiative and downward action:

> We believe that as we therefore love Christ, as John saith, because he first loved us (1 John 4:10), and we come unto him by our spirit, because he came first unto us by his, and therefore we embrace him by faith because he first, by virtue of his Spirit embracing us, stirs us up to faith, so we also can by no means cleave and be united unto him, unless he first joins and unites himself unto us. For the one is the cause of the other, the first of the latter.[6]

We ought to be united to Christ because he was first united to us. Or rather, the way redemption is stored up in Christ for us is by his

4. Zanchi, *Confession*, 231.
5. Zanchi, *Confession*, 233.
6. Zanchi, *Confession*, 233.

Union with Christ and the Christian Life   127

taking up human nature. He died for our sins in that nature united to himself and rose for our glorification in that nature united to himself. Because of that incarnational union, we are urged to seek another union—that is, the incorporation of our own persons into that work. Both unions are part of the one differentiated action of salvation being deposited in and dispensed from Christ.

In fact, once Zanchi has begun distinguishing these unions, he goes one step further. The incarnate/sacrificial union is the necessary presupposition of the union of faithful reception and is crowned by the union of glorification. The three unions are nested:

> We acknowledge furthermore this conjunction of Christ with us and likewise of us with Christ to be threefold: one, which was once made in our nature; another, which is daily made in the persons of the elect, which yet go astray from the Lord; and the last, which shall be likewise with the Lord in our persons when they shall be present with him, namely, when God shall be all in us all. And the first is referred to the second and the second to the third, even as nature is ordained to grace and grace to glory.[7]

The threefold union is not quite the same as the orders of nature, grace, and glory. After all, the incarnation and death of Christ can hardly be said to belong to the order of nature. But the three unions are ordered to each other in a way analogous to the way nature is ordered to grace, and grace to glory. The incarnate Son's redeeming work is ordered to bringing about and establishing the church's union with Christ, and that imperfect union with Christ is ordered to its perfect fulfillment in the presence of God.

These unions are nested so that each finds its fulfillment in the more complete one. "For the first [union] is made by assuming of our nature into the unity of the person the *logos*, of the Word." Zanchi emphasizes here the objective accomplishment of salvation, as the hypostasis of the Son assuming our nature. It is, in this sense, a union

7. Zanchi, *Confession*, 235.

of his person with our nature. But the second union is "made by assuming of our persons into grace and into one mystical body with him and, as Peter says, into participation of his divine nature."[8] The application or dispensing of salvation is, in this sense, a union of our persons with his nature. Zanchi here alludes to 2 Peter 1:4 with its famous promise of participation in the divine nature ("that . . . you may become partakers of the divine nature"). It is indeed a "great and precious promise," and Zanchi intends it to register as such. Salvation by grace in one sense answers analogously to the incarnation: Christ took on our nature so we could take on his.[9] The third and consummating union, in turn, "shall likewise be made by assuming of us all into everlasting glory with Christ."[10]

Zanchi's vision of union with Christ is obviously an expansive one. In sketching it out, we are in danger of launching out again into an all-encompassing trinitarian soteriology, with its sweeping horizons and dizzyingly high ceiling. But his crucial contribution for the subject of the Christian life is in his focus on the way salvation is worked out with a foundational integrity in Christ himself. That foundational integrity is what the Christian life is based on.

The Gospel Mystery of Sanctification

For a theology of the Christian life that is consistently and self-consciously grounded in union with Christ, we can do no better

---

8. Zanchi, *Confession*, 235. See also the sixth thesis on the same page: "As the first union was made that satisfaction might be made for our sins, so the second is made, that we might be partakers of that satisfaction."

9. This classic "exchange formula," made most famous perhaps by Athanasius, goes back at least to Irenaeus (*Against Heresies*, preface to book 5).

10. Zanchi, *Confession*, 235. Though I am drawing on Zanchi's *Confession*, his more famous work on union with Christ came from his work on Ephesians. What began as an elaborate doctrinal aside in his massive Ephesians commentary was published separately as an influential treatise, only recently made available in English translation by Patrick O'Banion: see Zanchi, *Spiritual Marriage between Christ and His Church and Every One of the Faithful*. J. V. Fesko notes that "very few early modern theologians devoted a specific locus to the doctrine of union with Christ, which makes this work a standout" and an influential reference point for later authors (Fesko, *Giver of Life*, 133).

than to turn to the Puritan pastoral theologian Walter Marshall (1628–80). Marshall's only published book bears the title *The Gospel Mystery of Sanctification*,[11] and though it has a great reputation (frequently praised in superlatives by those who know it), it still has not had as widespread an influence as it deserves. Marshall's writing style is both intense and prolix. He deeply loves his subject matter and spends three hundred pages devoutly expounding and applying a set of ideas that he has already established in outline in a dozen key pages. His idea of clear organization rarely matches the needs of the reader. But the spiritual insight at the heart of his classic book deserves close attention because it sets out the doctrine of union with Christ as the foundation of the entire Christian life.

Marshall uses the old word "sanctification" in a very broad sense, as an umbrella term that covers the life and experience of Christians. Of course it signifies holiness, and the holiness of Christians in particular (rather than the divine attribute proper). But Marshall especially emphasizes two aspects of sanctification. First, he focuses on the entire field of Christian life subsequent to conversion. That is, he is not thinking of conversion, the entrance into the Christian life, or a single experiential moment thereafter. Sanctification denotes a process, not a crisis; it is not a birth into life, but a lifetime. Second, he uses the term "sanctification" to indicate real changes experienced in that lifetime. That is, sanctification is not about a forensic reality, something considered as reckoned to a believer; it is not just a description of a new relation but an account of the actual difference that new relation makes in the ongoing life of the believer. If we bear in mind this usage (sanctification is a process of real change after conversion), then it is clear that we are talking, in somewhat old-fashioned terms, about the Christian life as it is actually lived out. And it is within that framework that Marshall brings out the centrality of union with Christ.

---

11. The work was originally published posthumously in 1692, and there are many subsequent editions with considerable editorial attempts to improve it. It is a tortuous editorial history! I am citing an edition (Zondervan, 1954) that I hope is relatively easy to find and has few alterations.

Although we are mostly calling on Marshall as the classic witness to the close fit between union with Christ and sanctification, we cannot understand his project without at least briefly noting his orientation toward the law. Marshall's *Gospel Mystery* presupposes a positive and constructive relation to the law of God, which he looks to as the standard of holiness within the Christian life. Unlike some other Christian schools of thought, Marshall's version of Reformed piety does not consider the law's main work to be driving us to the gospel. Instead, the law is an expression toward humanity of God's own holy character, and it only enters into its true and full work when it begins to bring about an actual change in the life of the believer. John Webster once declared that only by giving "a sketch of the individual Christian's sanctification" can a theology of holiness "trace to its end the trajectory of the work of the triune God."[12] Walter Marshall would put this more in terms of the law, but that is because he so closely identifies law and holiness. To trace the trajectory of the Trinity's transformative holiness to its end, Marshall might say, we must understand how the Father, Son, and Holy Spirit bring about the gospel mystery of obedient creatures.

What would it take for a creature to be obedient? This way of putting the question is distinctive; it is not the way everyone would approach sanctification. But once Marshall has guided his readers to see that it is the right question, he gives his answer: "The way to get holy endowments and qualifications necessary to frame and enable us for the immediate practice of the law, is to receive them out of the fulness of Christ, by fellowship with Him; and, that we may have this fellowship, we must be in Christ, and have Christ Himself in us, by a mystical union with Him."[13] The goal is to be empowered to live in holiness—that is, to acquire "qualifications necessary to . . . enable us for the immediate practice of the law." The way to that goal is mystical union with Christ.

12. Webster, *Holiness*, 7.
13. Marshall, *Gospel Mystery*, 27. This is the main text of what Marshall calls "Direction III" in his organizational plan for the book.

Union with Christ and the Christian Life

It is easy to imagine two objections to this formula. Legalists might object that the way to do the law is simply to do the law, not to change the subject to mystical union. That objection leads directly to Pelagianism, however. By contrast, all that Marshall is saying is that sanctification depends on a prior reality of salvation—he prefers to focus on union with Christ as the prerequisite, where a more conventional Protestant move might be to focus on justification as the prerequisite. On the other side, antinomians might object that Marshall's formulation demotes union with Christ, making it a means to a higher end, and thus treats the law as something greater than union with Christ. But Marshall is not saying that union with Christ exists solely for the purpose of bringing about righteous conduct; he is only saying that when we ask how to behave righteously, we will necessarily have to take the route of union with Christ. For that matter, mystical union might well be an end in itself. But then again, if a claim to union with Christ were to produce something besides obedience to the law, there would be reason to suspect it as illusory. Marshall hopes to redirect both kinds of objectors by showing them not only that holy living is the appropriate outcome of union with Christ, but that union with Christ is provided as the way to reach the goal of holy living. This is the mystery in the book's title, *The Gospel Mystery of Sanctification*.

A key word for Marshall is "frame," which he uses in the sense of the way a soul is composed or comported toward things. A frame is a disposition or habitual attitude, more or less settled. Marshall uses the word to indicate the mental, emotional, and spiritual state of readiness a believer must be in to behave properly. His eye is always on conduct and practical behavior, but he does not ignore the condition of the mind and heart, the character from which these outward actions arise. Behind and beneath our conduct is a "holy frame and disposition, by which our souls are furnished and enabled for immediate practice of the law."[14] This frame is not something we compose for ourselves. Rather, it "must be obtained by receiving it

14. Marshall, *Gospel Mystery*, 27.

out of Christ's fulness, as a thing already prepared and brought to an existence for us in Christ and treasured up in Him; and that as we are justified by a righteousness wrought out in Christ and imputed to us, so we are sanctified by such a holy frame and qualifications as are first wrought out and completed in Christ for us, and then imparted to us."[15] Marshall is using a schema here that we can recognize from Zanchi: our holiness is treasured up in Christ, where it was first created in him for us. The holiness we need was completed in him to be imparted to us. Marshall extends Zanchi's deposited-dispensed schema even more deeply into Christian experience.

The new life of believers runs in parallel to the old: "As our natural corruption was produced originally in the first Adam, and propagated from him to us, so our new nature and holiness is first produced in Christ, and derived from Him to us, or, as it were, propagated."[16] Marshall's emphasis is on the fact that the "holy frame" we require is itself a thing established outside of us, for our later appropriation. "We are not at all to work together with Christ, in making or producing that holy frame in us, but only to take it to ourselves, and use it in our holy practice, as made ready to our hands."[17] Union with Christ includes the reception of "that holy frame of spirit that was originally in Him."[18] Marshall takes for granted that his readers clearly understand justification by grace through faith and that they are accustomed to reckoning that the work of Christ is imputed to them for forgiveness of sins. His goal is to draw out the deeper reality supporting this imputation and to bring it into Christian experience.

We commonly think that we must get a holy frame, by producing it anew in ourselves, and by forming and working it out of our own hearts. Therefore many that are seriously devout, take a great deal of pains to mortify their corrupt nature, and beget a holy frame of heart

15. Marshall, *Gospel Mystery*, 27.
16. Marshall, *Gospel Mystery*, 27–28.
17. Marshall, *Gospel Mystery*, 28.
18. Marshall, *Gospel Mystery*, 28.

in themselves, by striving earnestly to master their sinful lusts, and by pressing vehemently upon their hearts many motives to godliness, laboring importunately to squeeze good qualifications out of them as oil out of a flint. They account, that though they be justified by a righteousness wrought out by Christ, yet they must be sanctified by a holiness, wrought out by themselves. And though, out of humility, they are willing to call it *infused grace*, yet they think they must get the infusion of it by the same manner of working, as if it were wholly acquired by their own endeavors.[19]

A large part of Marshall's project is to ensure that justification by faith does not pivot to sanctification by works but rather bears fruit as sanctification by faith. And his confidence that this can happen comes from his steady vision of union with Christ as the comprehensive, underlying reality. This underlying reality is why we "receive a new nature out of the fulness of Christ."[20]

Marshall focuses attention on the "gospel mystery" and explains that its mysterious character is its mystic character—that is, the mystical union by which believers are spiritually joined to Christ himself. "I may well call this a *mystical union*, because the Apostle calls it a *great mystery*, in an epistle full of mysteries (Eph. 5:22), intimating, that it is eminently great above many other mysteries."[21] Readers should not be surprised by Marshall's next move: he says union with Christ

is one of the three mystical unions that are the chief mysteries in religion. The other two are, the union of the Trinity of Persons in one Godhead, and the union of the divine and human natures in one Person, Jesus Christ, God and man. Though we cannot frame an exact idea of the manner of any of these three unions in our imaginations, because the depth of these mysteries is beyond our comprehension, yet we have cause to believe them all, because they are clearly revealed

19. Marshall, *Gospel Mystery*, 28.
20. Marshall, *Gospel Mystery*, 28.
21. Marshall, *Gospel Mystery*, 29.

in Scripture, and are a necessary foundation for other points of Christian doctrine.[22]

The now familiar cascading mystery structure of the three unions is once again invoked here as the comprehensive reality of salvation. Together these three unions constitute the center of Christian theology, the basis on which other doctrines are constructed and comprehended.

To anchor his point even more securely, Marshall takes up the biblical story of the life of Jesus, indicating how the major moments in that life were devoted to preparing the "new holy frame" of obedience. That is, in order to speak more clearly about how sanctification is dispensed or distributed to believers, he first expounds how it was deposited, or stored up in, the life of Christ: "The end of Christ's incarnation, death, and resurrection, was to prepare and form a holy nature and frame for us in Himself, to be communicated to us by union and fellowship with Him; and not to enable us to produce in ourselves the first original of such a holy nature, by our own endeavors."[23] That frame was instituted in Christ and developed over the course of his earthly life. We see it at the level of the incarnation itself:

> By his incarnation, there was a man created in a new holy frame, after the holiness of the first Adam's frame that had been marred and abolished by the first transgression; and this new frame was far more excellent than ever the first Adam's was; because man was really joined to God by a close, inseparable union of the divine and human nature in one person, Christ.[24]

We see it further in his death, by which "He freed Himself from the guilt of our sins, imputed to Him, and from all that innocent weakness of His human nature, which He had borne for a time for

22. Marshall, *Gospel Mystery*, 29.
23. Marshall, *Gospel Mystery*, 34.
24. Marshall, *Gospel Mystery*, 34.

Union with Christ and the Christian Life

135

our sakes."[25] By dealing with our sins by his own death, Christ "prepared a freedom for us, from our whole natural condition; which is both weak as His was, and also polluted with our guilt and sinful corruption."[26] Finally, we see it in his resurrection, by which "He took possession of spiritual life for us, as now fully procured for us, and made to be our right and property by the merit of His death,"[27] which is why believers are described in Ephesians 2:5 as "made alive together with Christ" and raised up to sit in heavenly places in him. "His resurrection was our resurrection to the life of holiness, as Adam's fall was our fall into spiritual death."[28]

After a brief theological survey of the way Christ worked out this new holy frame of obedience on our behalf, Marshall turns to the work of the Holy Spirit in dispensing it to us. But his pivot to that theological point is to argue that even the power of the Holy Spirit was first and foremost worked out on our behalf in the life of Jesus: "The Holy Ghost first rested on Christ in all fulness, that He might be communicated from Him to us,"[29] with the consequence that "according to the scriptural phrase, it is all one, to have Christ himself, and to have the Spirit of Christ, in us (Rom. 8:9, 10). . . . He giveth us an experimental knowledge of those spiritual blessings which he himself prepared for us by the incarnation, death, and resurrection of Christ."[30] Marshall's Christ-centered account of sanctification by faith does not exclude or distract from the work of the Spirit; in fact it drives toward a pneumatological consummation with considerable force.

God's Work for Us, God's Work in Us

We have traced a movement from Zanchi (grace deposited and dispensed) through Marshall (a holy frame of obedience placed in

25. Marshall, *Gospel Mystery*, 35.
26. Marshall, *Gospel Mystery*, 35.
27. Marshall, *Gospel Mystery*, 36.
28. Marshall, *Gospel Mystery*, 36.
29. Marshall, *Gospel Mystery*, 36.
30. Marshall, *Gospel Mystery*, 36–37.

Christ for us) by way of the comprehensiveness of union with Christ. In such massively Christocentric approaches to soteriology, there is always a lingering temptation to fail to give appropriate attention to the Father and the Holy Spirit. Though we have taken care to show how the Christocentric impulse coheres with a fully trinitarian faith, it is worth concluding with some more direct attention to the Holy Spirit.

A classic text in the evangelical tradition that takes up this task is Bonar's *Kelso Tracts*. While pastoring in Kelso, Scotland, in the 1840s, Horatius Bonar (1808–89) occasionally published little pamphlets, between three and twelve pages long, just to reach his local audience. Though he initially intended them only as written "helps to his own pastoral work," without "any ambitious aim of writing for a wider circle," they proved popular beyond his own congregation.[31] He gathered thirty-seven of these and published them under the title of *Kelso Tracts*; in this form they became a minor evangelical masterpiece of spiritual theology. Such an assemblage of tracts is bound to range over a lot of different subjects, and their themes are predictably broad as a survey of the things Bonar found it necessary to preach and teach during his ministry in Kelso. But Bonar had a well-organized mind and a definite focus as an evangelical pastor. As a result, in the preface he is able to summarize the "leading object" of his work: "The leading object of the whole Series may be said to be, to endeavour to bring out with some fulness, perhaps with some repetition, the Work of Christ, and the Work of the Holy Spirit, in reference to the wants of sinners."[32] In other words, Bonar's idea of effective gospel ministry is carefully structured by an applied evangelical trinitarianism. In particular, the *Kelso Tracts* show his concern to take in the comprehensive character of the Christian life by way of a careful distinction

---

31. Bonar, *Kelso Tracts*. The bound volume runs to about three hundred pages, but its original editions didn't have continuous page numbering: the page count started over with each tract, reinforcing their origin as individual booklets. A few of the tracts are actually republications of older authors (Becon, Baxter, Whitefield) in a form Bonar could easily distribute.

32. Bonar, *Kelso Tracts*, iv–v.

Union with Christ and the Christian Life   137

between the work of the Son and the work of the Holy Spirit. Bonar found that "in conversation with the troubled and doubting... much confusion prevailed in their minds, as to both of these points, the Work of Christ, and the Work of the Spirit."[33]

Bonar's Son-Spirit way of stating the insight was once prominent in Protestant spirituality but has since been all but forgotten, so it is worth quoting at length.

> There seemed a continual tendency to intermingle these two things, and so to subvert both; to build for eternity, partly on the one, and partly on the other, and so to come short of any true and sure establishment of the soul in grace. Many seemed most perversely bent on taking these two works as if they were one compounded work, trying to build their peace, their forgiveness, their salvation, upon a mysterious mixture of the two. The external and the internal were not kept distinct; the objective and the subjective were confusedly tangled together, so that neither was understood aright, and both were misapplied. It was not CHRIST FOR US, AND THE HOLY SPIRIT IN US, but it was Christ and the Holy Spirit together, both for us and in us. Thus, all was vagueness and indistinctness in reference to what Christ had done, and in reference to what the Holy Spirit had been sent down to do. Hence, all was darkness in the soul. There was no peace, for the ground of peace was not rightly seen; there was no holiness, for the source of holiness was but imperfectly apprehended. This Popish mixture of these two things—"Christ for us, and the Spirit in us," required to be exposed to view, its unscripturalness condemned, and its evil influence neutralized.[34]

What Bonar traces here could of course be paraphrased; it could be stated more Christocentrically as a distinction between what Christ himself did for us and what Christ himself goes on to do in us. Bonar's Christ-Spirit distinction could, in other words, be considered as two aspects of our union and communion with Christ. But there is also

33. Bonar, *Kelso Tracts*, v.
34. Bonar, *Kelso Tracts*, introduction.

wisdom in following the logic of trinitarian appropriation and identifying the external work with the Son and the internal work with the mission of the Holy Spirit. That way of distributing the emphases means that our minds will be instructed in trinitarian dynamics at the same time as we learn where to look for assurance: "It is CHRIST FOR US, that is our peace. It is THE HOLY SPIRIT IN US, that is our regeneration and holiness. Woe be to the soul that intermingles these two, and seeks to rest his peace and hope, partly on what Christ had done for him, and partly on what the Spirit is doing in him."[35]

What currently resides in the Christian mind as a muddy mixture must be theologically sorted in a pastorally helpful way. The work of Christ and the Spirit must both be made thematic so that they can be distinguished and then coordinated. Bonar explains a bit more:

> It is only, then, by setting distinctly forth the Work of Christ for us, and the Work of the Spirit in us, that we can really present the sinner with what he needs. As absolutely helpless and unholy, he needs an Almighty Spirit to new-create him. As condemned and accursed, he needs a Divine substitute and peace-maker. And in making known the latter, we preach the Gospel. For the Gospel is the good news of what another has done for us. . . . And in setting forth the work of the Spirit, we are called upon to be careful, on the one hand, to show the necessity for the direct and special operation of His power; and on the other, to guard the sinner against resting upon the Spirit's work, as if it were part of the foundation on which he builds for heaven. The work in us, however deep and decisive, can never pacify our consciences or reconcile us to God. It can never make, or maintain, our peace. It cannot be our resting place, or our Saviour.[36]

Bonar thinks of this ordered reciprocity of the Son and the Spirit as the structure that enables us to speak meaningfully of all that is

---

35. Bonar, *Kelso Tracts*, vi; there follows in a footnote a long quotation from John Owen on the same subject.
36. Bonar, *Kelso Tracts*, vii–viii.

Union with Christ and the Christian Life

139

in salvation; it is in some sense the "tangible shape" of the message in its integrity:

> It is of the utmost moment that these things be attended to, otherwise we shall never present the Gospel in any really tangible shape. Nay, we shall so confound things that differ, that they to whom it is preached shall not be able to see in it any glad tidings at all. With much that is evangelical, both in phrase and sentiment, in our statements, we may yet miss the real point and burden of the Gospel, and so leave men nearly as much in the dark as if we had set them upon providing a righteousness for themselves.[37]

This structural observation is especially significant. Without the trinitarian background operating at least subliminally for the teacher, pastoral speech can turn into a shambles, with bits and pieces of gospel truth jostling around but never hanging together. The resulting word salad may be quite spiritual, but it is formless. It can be a kind of high-energy static containing confused fragments of truth.

To take the renewing work of the indwelling Spirit as the basis of salvation is "an entire inversion of God's order."[38] The only way to embrace the work of the Son and the Spirit is to observe the distinction and correlation between them. Premature harmonization of the two is really just pervasive confusion of the two. The result is a sophisticated form of seeking justification by works: "It ends with securing forgiveness, whereas God's religion begins with securing it."[39]

Trinitarian Soteriology in Christ

The line of thought we have traced from Zanchi to Marshall to Bonar is markedly Protestant, and though these authors are international in origin and influence, and catholic in scope, the overall drift of

---

37. Bonar, *Kelso Tracts*, ix.
38. Bonar, *Kelso Tracts*, x.
39. Bonar, *Kelso Tracts*, x.

this movement of thought is recognizably evangelical. Other trajectories could have been traced through Roman Catholic and Eastern Orthodox communions, making many (though not all) of the same points in characteristic accents, taking on local color. In a longer book, several of them could be explored one after another and then brought into explicit dialogue with one another. It would be a great and sweeping project to gather up and consider together all the ways of understanding and articulating what it means to be in Christ. But in a book of this length, strict selections have to be made, and only a few related trajectories can be traced. And although the entire book has considered the notion of union with Christ from the broadest possible perspective in creedal and canonical context, to speak about these widely shared things under the heading of "union with Christ" is nevertheless to speak in a somewhat Protestant idiom, and with a rather evangelical accent. The thing itself is essentially Christian: it describes a doctrine of salvation that is catholic and orthodox and evangelical in the adjectival, nonproprietary sense of these good old terms. But calling it "union with Christ" suggests that the speaker has probably already read some Puritans.

Still, it would be good to bring the argument to a close with a gesture toward the shared theology of the great church. Toward that end, I call as a witness Irenaeus of Lyons. I do not consider him to be a supporting witness for the precise way I have articulated union with Christ as trinitarian soteriology in these pages. For one thing, Irenaeus's theology was animated by different worries; the challenges he answered in his time were not the same as ours. For another thing, he saw so far into the depth of all these matters that we ought to consider how we can support his witness to reality rather than he ours. But having traced the trinitarian soteriology of union with Christ to its termination in the experience of the Christian life, we are in a position to benefit afresh from hearing Irenaeus's way of putting things:

> For it was for this end that the Word of God was made man, and He who was the Son of God became the Son of man, that man, having

Union with Christ and the Christian Life

been taken into the Word, and receiving the adoption, might become the son of God. For by no other means could we have attained to incorruptibility and immortality, unless we had been united to incorruptibility and immortality. But how could we be joined to incorruptibility and immortality, unless, first, incorruptibility and immortality had become that which we also are, so that the corruptible might be swallowed up by incorruptibility, and the mortal by immortality, that we might receive the adoption of sons?[40]

In order to bring about this great exchange, the Son of the Father, through the Holy Spirit, came into fellowship with humanity, the Holy Spirit "becoming accustomed in fellowship with [the incarnate Son] to dwell in the human race, to rest with human beings, and to dwell in the workmanship of God, working the will of the Father in them, and renewing them from their old habits into the newness of Christ."[41] What Walter Marshall describes as the Son creating the frame in which we can live out lives of sanctification, Irenaeus long ago described more expansively as the incorruptible Son becoming what we are so that we might become what he is and share in his incorruptibility. The ancient author speaks relatively more metaphysically, the early modern author relatively more ethically. But between them they stake out the vast expanse of the one Christian doctrine of salvation by union with Christ. Salvation is in Christ because God and humanity are in Christ; the saving God is there, together with the humanity "new framed" for eternal fellowship with him.

40. Irenaeus, *Against Heresies* 3.19.1.
41. Irenaeus, *Against Heresies* 3.17.1.

DOXOLOGICAL POSTLUDE

"Thou Hidden Source" (Wesley)

Thou hidden source of calm repose,
Thou all sufficient love divine,
My help and refuge from my foes,
Secure I am if you are mine:
And lo! From sin, and grief, and shame
I hide me, Jesus, in thy name.

Thy mighty name salvation is,
And keeps my happy soul above;
Comfort it brings, and power, and peace,
And joy, and everlasting love:
To me, with your dear name are given
Pardon, and holiness, and heaven.

Jesus, my all in all thou art:
My rest in toil, my ease in pain,
The medicine of my broken heart,
In war my peace, in loss my gain.
My smile beneath the tyrant's frown,
In shame my glory and my crown.

In want my plentiful supply,
In weakness my almighty power,
In bonds my perfect liberty,
My light in Satan's darkest hour,
In grief my joy unspeakable,
My life in death, my heaven in hell.[1]

1. As found in Kimbrough, *Lyrical Theology of Charles Wesley*, 124–25.

Bibliography

Abernethy, Andrew. "Genre and Theological Vision." In *Interpreting the Old Testament Theologically: Essays in Honor of Willem A. VanGemeren*, edited by Andrew T. Abernethy, 43–56. Zondervan, 2018.

Ambrose, Isaac. *Looking unto Jesus: A View of the Everlasting Gospel, or, The Soul's Eyeing of Jesus, as Carrying Out the Great Work of Man's Salvation, from First to Last*. Lippincott, 1856.

Athanasius the Great and Didymus the Blind. *Works on the Spirit*. Translated by Mark DelCogliano, Andrew Radde-Gallwitz, and Lewis Ayres. Popular Patristics. St. Vladimir's Seminary Press, 2011.

Augustine. *Homilies on the Gospel of John, 1–40*. Translated by Edmund Hill. Works of Saint Augustine III/12. New City, 2009.

Baker, Mark D., and Joel B. Green. *Recovering the Scandal of the Cross: Atonement in New Testament and Contemporary Contexts*. 2nd ed. IVP Academic, 2011.

Beilby, James, and Paul R. Eddy. *The Nature of the Atonement: Four Views*. IVP Academic, 2006.

Bennema, Cornelis. "'Union with Christ' in the Johannine Writings." In *In Christ Alone: Perspectives on Union with Christ*, edited by Stephen Clark and Matthew Evans, 17–44. Christian Focus Publications, 2016.

Bernard of Clairvaux. *On the Song of Songs*. 4 vols. Cistercian Publications, 1971–80.

Bonar, Horatius. *Kelso Tracts*. James Nisbet, 1851.

Bowsher, Clive. *Life in the Son: Exploring Participation and Union with Christ in John's Gospel and Letters*. InterVarsity, 2023.

Bruce, F. F. *Paul: Apostle of the Heart Set Free*. Eerdmans, 2000.

Calvin, John. *Institutes of the Christian Religion*. Edited by John T. McNeill. Translated by Ford Lewis Battles. 2 vols. Westminster, 1960.

Campbell, Constantine. *Paul and Union with Christ: An Exegetical and Theological Study*. Zondervan, 2012.

Carter, Jonathan M. *Thomas Goodwin on Union with Christ: The Indwelling of the Spirit, Participation in Christ and the Defence of Reformed Soteriology*. T&T Clark, 2022.

Dixon, Philip. *Nice and Hot Disputes: The Doctrine of the Trinity in the Seventeenth Century*. T&T Clark, 2003.

Ferguson, Sinclair. *The Holy Spirit*. InterVarsity, 1996.

Fesko, J. V. "The Communion Controversy: Owen and Sherlock on 'Union with Christ.'" In *In Christ Alone: Perspectives on Union with Christ*, edited by Stephen Clark and Matthew Evans, 118–50. Christian Focus Publications, 2016.

———. *The Giver of Life: The Biblical Doctrine of the Holy Spirit and Salvation*. Lexham Academic, 2024.

———. "Romans 8.29–30 and the Question of the *Ordo Salutis*." *Journal of Reformed Theology* 8 (2014): 35–60.

Gaffin, Richard B., Jr. *By Faith, Not by Sight: Paul and the Order of Salvation*. 2nd ed. P&R, 2013.

Garcia, Mark A. *Life in Christ: Union with Christ and Twofold Grace in Calvin's Theology*. Paternoster, 2008.

Gates, Henry Louis, Jr., ed. *Frederick Douglass: Autobiographies*. Library of America, 1994.

Goodwin, Thomas. *Christ Set Forth in His Death, Resurrection, Ascension, Sitting at God's Right Hand, Intercession [. . .]*. Vol. 4 of *The Works of Thomas Goodwin*. James Nichol, 1862.

———. *Containing an Exposition of Various Passages of the Epistle to the Ephesians; and Patience and Its Perfect Work, Being an Exposition of James 1:1–5*. Vol. 2 of *The Works of Thomas Goodwin*. James Nichol, 1861. Reprint, Reformation Heritage Books, 2006.

———. *The Object and Acts of Justifying Faith*. Vol. 8 of *The Works of Thomas Goodwin*. James Nichol, 1864.

Green, Rosalie, and Isa Ragusa. *Meditations on the Life of Christ: An Illustrated Manuscript of the Fourteenth Century*. 2nd ed. Princeton University Press, 1961.

Bibliography

Gregory of Nyssa. *On "Not Three Gods."* In *Nicene and Post-Nicene Fathers*, Series 2, edited by Philip Schaff and Henry Wace, 5:331–36. Reprint, Eerdmans, 1954.

Grillmeier, Aloys. "Mit ihm und in ihm: Das Mysterium und die Mysterien Christi." In *Mit ihm und in ihm: Christologische Forschungen und Perspektiven*, 716–35. Herder, 1975.

Guardini, Romano. *The Lord*. Regnery, 1954.

Hall, Joseph. *Contemplations on the Historical Passages of the Old and New Testaments*. Thomas Nelson, 1844.

Holland, H. S. "Criticism and the Resurrection." In *On Behalf of Belief: Sermons Preached in St. Paul's Cathedral*, 1–24. Longmans, Green, 1892.

Hood, Jason B. *Imitating God in Christ: Recapturing a Biblical Pattern*. InterVarsity, 2013.

Horton, Michael. *Calvin on the Christian Life: Glorifying and Enjoying God Forever*. Crossway, 2014.

Irenaeus of Lyons. *Against Heresies*. In *Ante-Nicene Fathers*, edited by Alexander Roberts and James Donaldson, translated by Alexander Roberts, 1:309–567. Reprint, Eerdmans, n.d.

Johnson, Adam. *Atonement and the Life of Faith*. Soteriology and Doxology. Baker Academic, 2024.

———. "Theories and *Theoria* of the Atonement: A Proposal." *International Journal of Systematic Theology* 23, no. 1 (2021): 92–108.

Julian, John. *A Dictionary of Hymnology*. John Murray, 1892.

Kähler, Martin. *The So-Called Historical Jesus and the Historic, Biblical Christ*. Fortress, 1964.

Kelly, J. N. D. *Early Christian Doctrines*. Rev. ed. Harper & Row, 1978.

Kimbrough, S. T., Jr. *The Lyrical Theology of Charles Wesley: A Reader*. 3rd ed. Lutterworth Press, 2014.

Legge, Dominic. *The Trinitarian Christology of St. Thomas Aquinas*. Oxford University Press, 2017.

Lim, Paul C. H. *Mystery Unveiled: The Crisis of the Trinity in Early Modern England*. Oxford University Press, 2012.

Litton, E. A. *Introduction to Dogmatic Theology: On the Basis of the Thirty-Nine Articles*. 3rd ed. Robert Scott, 1912.

Longenecker, Bruce W., ed. *Narrative Dynamics in Paul: A Critical Assessment*. Westminster John Knox, 2002.

Machen, J. Gresham. *Christianity and Liberalism*. Macmillan, 1923.

Marshall, Walter. *The Gospel Mystery of Sanctification*. Zondervan, 1954.

Martin, Hugh. *The Abiding Presence*. Christian Focus Publications, 2009.

Mastricht, Petrus van. *Theoretical-Practical Theology*. Vol. 2, *Faith in the Triune God*. Reformation Heritage Books, 2019.

———. *Theoretical-Practical Theology*. Vol. 4, *Redemption in Christ*. Reformation Heritage Books, 2023.

McFarland, Ian A. "'God, the Father Almighty': A Theological Excursus." *International Journal of Systematic Theology* 18, no. 3 (July 2016): 259–73.

McNall, Joshua. *The Mosaic of Atonement: An Integrated Approach to Christ's Work*. Zondervan Academic, 2019.

Morgan, G. Campbell. *The Crises of the Christ*. Fleming H. Revell, 1903.

Muller, Richard A. *Dictionary of Latin and Greek Theological Terms: Drawn Principally from Protestant Scholastic Theology*. 2nd ed. Baker Academic, 2017.

Murray, John. *Redemption Accomplished and Applied*. Eerdmans, 1955.

Newman, John Henry. *Sermons, Chiefly on the Theory of Religious Belief, Preached Before the University of Oxford*. Rivington, 1843.

O'Byrne, Declan. *"For Us and for Our Salvation": The "Christological" Councils and Trinitarian Anthropology*. Urbaniana University Press, 2018.

Owen, John. *Of Communion with God the Father, Son, and Holy Ghost, Each Person Distinctly, in Love, Grace, and Consolation*. In *Works of John Owen*, 2:5–274. Edited by William H. Goold. Johnstone & Hunter, 1850.

Pierson, A. T. *In Christ Jesus, or, The Sphere of the Believer's Life*. Funk & Wagnalls, 1898.

Polhill, Edward. *An Answer to the Discourse of Mr. William Sherlock, Touching the Knowledge of Christ and Our Union and Communion with Him*. B. Foster, 1675.

———. *Christus in Corde, or, The Mystical Union Between Christ and Believers Considered in Its Resemblances, Bonds, Seals, Privileges and Marks*. Thomas Cockerill, 1680.

———. *Speculum Theologiae in Christo*. In *The Works of Edward Polhill*, 1–109. Thomas Ward and Co., 1844.

Radde-Gallwitz, Andrew, ed. *The Cambridge Edition of Early Christian Writings*. Vol. 1, *God*. Cambridge University Press, 2017.

Ratzinger, Joseph. *Jesus of Nazareth*. 3 vols. Doubleday, 2007–12.

Ryle, J. C. "Evangelical Religion." In *Knots Untied: Being Plain Statements on Disputed Points in Religion from the Standpoint of an Evangelical Churchman*. William Hunt, 1885.

Sanders, Fred. "Biblical Grounding for the Christology of the Councils." *Criswell Theological Review* 13, no. 1 (Fall 2015): 93–104.

Saphir, Adolph. *Christ and the Church: Thoughts on the Apostolic Commission*. Religious Tract Society, 1884.

Sherlock, William. *A Discourse Concerning the Knowledge of Jesus Christ, and Our Union and Communion with Him*. Walter Kettilby, 1674.

Stier, Rudolf. *The Words of Jesus*. Translated by William B. Pope. T&T Clark, 1861.

Taylor, Jeremy. *The Great Exemplar of Sanctity and Holy Life According to the Christian Institution: Described in the History of the Life and Death of the Ever Blessed Jesus Christ the Saviour of the World; With Considerations and Discourses Upon the Several Parts of the Story, and Prayers Fitted to the Several Mysteries*. Printed by R. N. for Francis Alb., 1649.

Thomas Aquinas. *Commentary on Saint Paul's Epistle to the Ephesians*. Translated by Matthew L. Lamb. Aquinas Scripture Series 2. Magi Books, 1966.

Thurston, Herbert. "Notes on Familiar Prayers, VII: The Anima Christi." *The Month* 125 (May 1915): 493–505.

Vanhoozer, Kevin. "From 'Blessed in Christ' to 'Being in Christ': The State of Union and the Place of Participation in Paul's Discourse, New Testament Exegesis, and Systematic Theology Today." In *"In Christ" in Paul: Explorations in Paul's Theology of Union and Participation*, edited by Michael J. Thate, Kevin J. Vanhoozer, and Constantine R. Campbell, 3–34. Mohr Siebeck, 2014.

———. *Is There a Meaning in This Text? The Bible, the Reader, and the Morality of Literary Knowledge*. Zondervan, 1998.

———. "The Semantics of Biblical Literature: Truth and Scripture's Diverse Literary Forms." In *Hermeneutics, Authority and Canon*, edited by D. A. Carson and John D. Woodbridge, 53–104. Inter-Varsity, 1986.

Webster, John. "Discovering Dogmatics." In *Shaping a Theological Mind: Theological Context and Methodology*, edited by Darren C. Marks, 129–36. Ashgate, 2002.

———. *God without Measure: Working Papers in Christian Theology*. 2 vols. T&T Clark, 2016.

———. *Holiness*. Eerdmans, 2002.

Weinandy, Thomas. *Jesus Becoming Jesus*. 3 vols. Catholic University of America Press, 2018–22.

Zanchi, Girolamo. *De religione christiana fides / Confession of Christian Religion*. Edited by Luca Baschera and Christian Moser. Brill, 2007.

———. *The Spiritual Marriage between Christ and His Church and Every One of the Faithful*. Translated by Patrick O'Banion. Reformation Heritage Books, 2021.

Scripture Index

Old Testament

Isaiah

52:6 85

New Testament

Matthew

11:27 113
28:19 113

John

1:3 19
1:4 107
2:19 81
6 75
10:18 81
14:16–17 107
14:23 107
15:1–7 126
15:5 66
17:21 10–11

Acts

10 14
27:17–18 92

Romans

5 29
6 29
8 29
8:9–10 135
8:17 46
8:28–30 92
8:29 58n5
8:29–30 97
11:17 58n5

1 Corinthians

1:30 47
1:30–31 46
11:23–24 47
15:3 49
15:3–4 47

2 Corinthians

4:10 77

Galatians

1:6–7 5
2:20 46, 77
3:27 58n5
4:4–5 113

Ephesians

1 39–40, 44
1:10 125

1:19 40
1:20 40–42, 44
2 29, 39–40, 42, 46n24
2:1 44
2:1–10 44
2:4–7 27
2:5 44, 45n22, 135
2:5–6 40–44, 112
2:6 45n22
2:7 44
2:8 42
3 75
4:15 58n5
5:22 133

Colossians

3:4 77

Hebrews

5:7 59n7

2 Peter

1:4 128

1 John

1:5 18
4:10 126
5:7 109

Subject Index

Note: The abbreviation UWC stands for "union with Christ."

Abiding Presence, The (Martin), 36–38
accomplished-applied schema, 93–99, 104, 105, 110, 124–25
Ambrose, Isaac, 78–82
Andrewes, Lancelot, 7, 9
Anglican Church, 7
Anima Christi, 1, 6–9
Anselm of Canterbury, 12, 98–99
Answer to the Discourse of Mr. William Sherlock, An (Polhill), 69–70
apocalyptic genre, 48
Apostles' Creed, 12–17, 18, 20, 54–56, 57–58
apostolic epistles. *See* epistles, apostolic
appropriation, 13
Aquinas, 74–76, 77, 101
Aspirations of St. Ignatius, 6
Athanasius, 101, 119n49, 128n9
atonement theology, 62–63, 98–103, 104, 110–11
Augustine, 75
Aulén, Gustaf, 103

Baur, F. C., 99–100, 101, 103
Bernard of Clairvaux, 66, 87
Bonar, Horatius, 121, 136–39
Bowsher, Clive, 48–49
Bruce, F. F., 46n23

Calvin, John, 47, 54–61, 101
Christ and the Church (Saphir), 51–52
Christian faith, 10–11, 17
Christian life, 123–41
  deposited-dispensed schema in, 125–28, 132, 135
  diversity in, 123
  Holy Spirit in, 135–39
  sanctification in, 128–35
  trinitarian context for, 139–41
  UWC consistent across, 123–24, 135
Christology
  of early church, 13–14, 18–20, 22, 80–81
  soteriology and, 113
  See also Jesus Christ; life of Christ
Christ Set Forth (Goodwin), 82–83
Christ's Presence in the Gospel Narrative (Martin), 36–38
Christus in Corde (Polhill), 70, 72, 89
church, 11, 66–67, 123–24. *See also* early church
Church of England, 62–63
Communion with God (Owen), 65–66, 87
comparative soteriology, 88
Confession of Christian Religion (Zanchi), 125
contemplation and meditation, 78–80, 83, 102, 104, 105
Contemplations on the Historical Passages of the Old and New Testaments (Hall), 84

153

154   Subject Index

Council of Chalcedon (451), 79
Council of Constantinople II (553), 79
creation, creedal theology of, 13, 18–19, 20
Creed of the Council of Constantinople,
    17n9
creeds, 3–25
    Apostles' Creed, 12–17, 18, 20, 54–56,
        57–58
    Calvin's soteriology and, 54–61
    Christian faith shaped by, 10–11, 17
    Christology of, 13–14, 18–20, 22, 80–81
    credibility of faith and, 10–11
    early soteriology in, 11–12, 15, 19, 21–22
    Nicene Creed, 17–22
    purpose of, 3
    Trinity articulated in, 11–12, 17, 19–20,
        21–22
    UWC and existence of, 17, 23, 25, 56
    UWC articulated by, 15–17, 20–22
Crises of the Christ, The (Morgan), 85–86
Cur deus homo (Anselm), 98

deposited-dispensed schema, 125–28, 132,
    135
"Die Seele Christi heil'ge mich" (Scheffler), 7
divine simplicity, 104
doctrine, history of, 99
"double grace," 47
Douglass, Frederick, 35–36
doxologies, 1, 6–9, 27, 51–52, 89, 121, 143

Early Christian Creeds (Kelly), 99
Early Christian Doctrines (Kelly), 99
early church
    Christology of, 13–14, 18–20, 22, 80–81
    soteriology of, 11–12, 15, 19, 21–22
    ecumenical councils, 10, 11, 12, 22, 80–81
Ephesians, book of, 39–45
epistles, apostolic
    as documents of UWC, 29, 39, 48
    Johannine, 48–49
    Pauline, 39–48
    structure of UWC in, 29–30, 39–47,
        48–50

Ferguson, Sinclair, 105
Fesko, J. V., 65n10, 69n19, 128n10

fittingness, logic of, 75
frame, holy, 131–33, 134, 135–36, 141

Gaffin, Richard, 104
genre, defined, 30
genres, New Testament, 29–52
    apocalyptic, 48–49
    apostolic epistles (*see* epistles, apostolic)
    as documents of UWC, 29, 39, 48
    Gospel, 31–39, 48–49
    structure of UWC in, 30, 39–45, 48, 49–50
genres and schemas for union with Christ,
    73–87
    commentary, 84–85, 87
    devotional writing, 78–84
    "from above," 86–87
    God's plan through Christ's work, 85–86
    "life of the mediator," 76–77
    meditation, 74, 82–83
    "mysteries of the life of Christ," 74–82,
        83–87
    narrative, 13–15, 16–17, 56, 77, 92
    ordo salutis, xiii, 92–97, 104, 105, 124
    words of Jesus, 84–85
God, creedal theology of, 12–13, 18–19
Goodwin, Thomas
    on actions of Christ, 82–83
    diminishment of UWC avoided by, 65
    on trinitarian agency, 114–15, 119–20
    on UWC in Ephesians, 43–45, 46nn24–25
Gospel, genre of, 31–39, 48–49
Gospel-first-then-epistle structure, 30, 39–45,
    48, 49–50
Gospel Mystery of Sanctification, The (Mar-
    shall), 129–35
grace deposited and dispensed, 125–28, 132,
    135
Great Exemplar, The (Taylor), 83–84
Green, Joel, 100n13
Gregory of Nyssa, 117

Hall, Joseph, 84
Holland, Henry Scott, 34
"holy frame," 131–33, 134, 135–36, 141
Holy Spirit
    in Calvin's soteriology, 56, 58–60
    Christian obedience and, 135–36

Subject Index

creedal theology of, 15–17
in Polhill's soteriology, 72–73
work of Christ and, 136–39
homoousios, 18
Horton, Michael, 57
hypostatic union, 71, 108, 109, 115,
127–28

"I Cannot Nearer Be" (Bonar), 121
Ignatius of Loyola, 6
incarnation
atonement and, 62–63
Christian life and, xiii, 134
creedal treatment of, 21–22
mystical union and, 71, 107–8, 127
trinitarian agency and, 115
"in Christ"
diminishment of, 64–70
OT version of, 49
Paul's use of, 29–30, 40–48
Scripture itself as, 50
as soteriological approach, xi–xii
structure of UWC summarized by, 30,
39–42, 44, 48, 50, 95
trinitarian context of, 120
inclusion in Christ
in creeds, 15–16, 21
in NT genres, 30, 40–42, 43–46, 112
OT witness to, 49
as redemption applied, 96
as second "moment" of UWC, xi–xii, 25,
40, 50, 74, 125
in theologies of UWC, 58, 60, 74
trinitarian foundation for, 115
Institutes of the Christian Religion (Calvin),
54–55, 56, 61
introspection, 83
Irenaeus of Lyons, 128n9, 140–41

"Jesu, Thy Soul Renew My Own" (Wesley),
7–9
Jesus Christ
hypostatic union and, 71, 81, 108, 115
initiative and action of, 126
names for, 14
trinitarian identity of, 17–22, 113–14,
120

work of Holy Spirit and, 136–39
See also life of Christ
John, writings of, 32, 48–49
Johnson, Adam, 99–101, 102, 103, 105

Kähler, Martin, 31
Kelly, J. N. D., 12, 21–22, 98–99, 101
Kelso Tracts (Bonar), 136–39

law, sanctification and, 130
Leontius of Byzantium, 80–81
Lewis, C. S., 53
Life and Times of Frederick Douglass, 35
life of Christ
Christian life shaped by, 123–24, 134–35,
141
creedal summaries of, 13–15, 16–17
as first "moment" of UWC, xi–xii, 25, 40,
50, 74, 125
in NT genres, 30, 31–32, 33–40, 47, 50, 77
OT witness to, 49
in theologies of UWC, 54, 56, 59, 60, 74
(*see also* "mysteries of the life of Christ"
genre)
"life of the mediator," 76–77
Litton, E. A., 62–63
Looking unto Jesus (Ambrose), 78–82, 92
Luke-Acts, 32
Lutheran Pietists, 7, 9

Machen, J. Gresham, 5
Mark, Gospel of, 31–32
Marshall, Walter, 129–35, 141
Martin, Hugh, 36–38
Mastricht, Petrus van, 76–78, 116–18
Matthew, Gospel of, 32–33
meditation and contemplation, 78–80, 83,
102, 104, 105
Meditations on the Life of Christ, 74n32
Morgan, G. Campbell, 85–86
Muller, Richard, 92
Murray, John, 21, 93–98, 105–7
My Bondage and My Freedom (Douglass), 35
"mysteries of the life of Christ" genre, 74–82,
83–87
mystical unions, 71, 105–11, 127–28,
133–34

Subject Index

narrative
  in creeds, 13–15, 16–17
  in NT genres, 31–32, 34, 35, 39, 50, 77
  in theologies of UWC, 54, 56, 59, 60, 74, 77, 92
  See also life of Christ
Narrative of the Life of Frederick Douglass, an American Slave, 35
Newman, John Henry, 34
New Testament. *See* Ephesians, book of; genres, New Testament
Nicene Creed, 17–22

obedience, 130, 134
Of Communion with God the Father, Son, and Holy Ghost (Owen), 87
oikonomia, 19, 21, 125
Old Testament, 49
ordo salutis, xiii, 92–97, 104, 105, 124–25
Owen, John, 65–66, 70, 87

Paget, Catesby, 121n1
Paul, soteriology of, 29–30, 39–48, 50
Pius IX (pope), 6
pneumatology, 15. *See also* Holy Spirit
Polhill, Edward, 69–73, 86–87, 89, 106, 109
Private Prayers (Andrewes), 7

redemption
  accomplished and applied schema of, 93–99, 104, 105, 110, 124–25
  creedal theology of, 16–17, 21
  deposited-dispensed schema of, 125–28, 132, 135
Redemption Accomplished and Applied (Murray), 93–99
Roman Catholic Church, 6–7, 8–9, 57, 62–63, 76

salvation, two moments of
  accomplished-applied schema for, 93–99, 104, 105, 110, 124–25
  deposited-dispensed schema for, 125–28, 132, 135
  as structure of UWC, xi–xii, 25, 40, 50, 74, 125
  See also inclusion in Christ; life of Christ

sanctification, 128–35
Saphir, Adolph, 51–52, 109–10
Scheffler, Johannes, 7
Scripture
  early church's response to (*see* creeds)
  inspiration of, 30
  Old Testament, 49
  See also genres, New Testament
Sherlock, William, 64–70
Song of Songs, commentaries on, 87
soteriology
  Christology and, 113
  comparative, 88
  in early church, 11–12, 15–17, 19, 21–22 (*see also* creeds)
  simplicity of, 104–5
  thinking and speaking rightly about, 4–6, 23–25, 62, 63
  trinitarian, 60, 93, 107, 128, 139–41
  UWC central to, xii–xiii, 4, 53, 62–63, 94
  See also union with Christ
Speculum Theologiae in Christo (Polhill), 86–87
Spiritual Exercises (Ignatius), 6
Stier, Rudolf, 84–85
Summa Theologiae (Thomas Aquinas), 74–77

Taylor, Jeremy, 83–84
theologia, 19, 21
theology, 24–25, 107–9
Theoretical-Practical Theology (Mastricht), 76–77
theoria, 102, 104, 105
Thirty-Nine Articles, 62
Thomas Aquinas, 74–76, 77, 101
"Thou Hidden Source" (Wesley), 143
three-unions schema, 71, 107–11, 127–28, 133–34
trinitarian soteriology, 60, 93, 107, 128, 139–41
Trinity, 91–122
  action of, 114–20
  in Bonar's *Kelso Tracts*, 136–39
  in Calvin's soteriology, 59–60
  creedal articulation of, 11–12, 17, 19–20, 21–22

Subject Index

in mystical unions, 71, 107–11, 133–34
trinitarian–Christocentric tension, 111–13,
  118–19, 120, 136

union, three mysteries of, 71, 107–11, 127–
  28, 133–34
union with Christ
  atonement theology and, 98, 102, 104, 111
  benefits of, 15–16, 47, 57, 72
  boundaries defining, 5–6, 8
  Christian life formed by (*see* Christian life)
  credibility of faith and, 10–11
  creedal articulation of, 15–17, 20–22
  defined, 96–97, 115
  diminishment of, 64–70
  "in Christ" language for, xi–xii, 30, 39–42,
    44, 48, 50, 95
  mysteries of, 105–11, 127–28, 130–31,
    133–34
  in New Testament (*see* epistles, apostolic;
    genres, New Testament)
  in Old Testament, 49
  sanctification and, 128–35
  scope and weight of, 63–64
  simplicity of, 104–5
  soteriology defined by, xii–xiii, 4, 53,
    62–63, 94
  structure of (*see* UWC, structure of)
  thinking and speaking rightly about, 4–6,
    23–25, 62, 63
  trinitarian nature of, 59–60, 93, 107, 128,
    139–41 (*see also* Trinity)
  variations on (*see* genres and schemas for
    UWC; UWC, variations on)
  writing about, 73–74, 88 (*see also* genres
    and schemas for UWC)

union with Christ, structure of
  accomplished and applied schema for, 17,
    93–99, 104, 105, 110, 124–25
  deposited and dispensed schema for,
    125–28, 132
  Gospel-first-then-epistle, 30, 39–45, 48,
    49–50, 77
  "in Christ" language for (*see* "in Christ")
  ordo salutis and, xiii, 92–97, 104, 105,
    124–25
  as trinitarian, xiii, 59–60 (*see also* Trinity)
  as two moments, xi–xii, 25, 40, 50, 125
union with Christ, variations on, 53–88
  assessing, 62, 63
  atonement theories and, 98–99
  boundaries containing, 5–6, 8, 64
  Calvin's creedal setting, 54–57
  natural diversity and, 53, 140
  Polhill's presentation, 70–73
  Protestant–Catholic differences, 6–9,
    62–63
  structural differences among, 57–63
  theological liberalism, 64–70
  See also genres and schemas for UWC

Vanhoozer, Kevin, 29–30, 104–5

*Way in Which We Receive the Grace of Christ,
  The* (Calvin), 61
Webster, John, 24, 102, 113–14, 130
Wesley, John, 7–8, 9, 143
Words of Jesus series (Stier), 84–85

Zanchi, Girolamo, 124–28, 132